EXPERIMENTS FOR FUTURE
ASTRONOMERS

EXPERIMENTS FOR FUTURE
ASTRONOMERS

**ROBERT GARDNER
AND JOSHUA CONKLIN**

Enslow Publishing
101 W. 23rd Street
Suite 240
New York, NY 10011
USA

enslow.com

Published in 2017 by Enslow Publishing, LLC.
101 W. 23rd Street, Suite 240, New York, NY 10011

Library of Congress Cataloging-in-Publication Data

Names: Gardner, Robert.
Title: Experiments for future astronomers / Robert Gardner and Joshua Conklin.
Description: New York : Enslow Publishing, 2017. | Series: Experiments for future STEM professionals | Includes bibliographical references and index.
Identifiers: ISBN 9780766082007 (library bound)
Subjects: LCSH: Astronomy—Experiments—Juvenile literature.
Classification: LCC QB61.G368 2017 | DDC 520—dc23

Printed in the United States of America

To Our Readers: We have done our best to make sure all website addresses in this book were active and appropriate when we went to press. However, the author and the publisher have no control over and assume no liability for the material available on those websites or on any websites they may link to. Any comments or suggestions can be sent by e-mail to customerservice@enslow.com.

Photo Credits: Cover, Alexander Raths/Shutterstock.com (man), Alexander Kolomietz/ Shutterstock.com (telescope), Yury Dmitrienko/Shutterstock.com (galaxy), Titov Nikolai/ Shutterstock.com (atom symbol), elic/Shutterstock.com (purple geometric background throughout book), Zffoto/Shutterstock.com (white textured background throughout book).

Illustrations by Joseph Hill.

CONTENTS

INTRODUCTION **8**

WHAT DO ASTRONOMERS DO? 11
THE SCIENTIFIC METHOD 12
BEFORE YOU BEGIN EXPERIMENTING 14
SAFETY FIRST 14

CHAPTER 1:
STELLAR CONSTELLATIONS:
SHAPES IN THE SKY..**17**

EXPERIMENT 1: THE BIG DIPPER, THE LITTLE DIPPER,
                AND A DIRECTION.............................. 18
EXPERIMENT 2: CAN A MAGNETIC COMPASS BE USED
                TO FIND TRUE NORTH? 21
EXPERIMENT 3: FINDING THE NORTH POLAR CONSTELLATIONS 22
EXPERIMENT 4: LOCATING THE NORTH POLAR CONSTELLATIONS
                OVER TIME IN HOURS 24
EXPERIMENT 5: OBSERVING THE NORTH POLAR CONSTELLATIONS
                OVER TIME IN MONTHS......................... 25

CHAPTER 2:
EARTH: ONE OF THE SUN'S SATELLITES **35**

EXPERIMENT 6: YOUR LATITUDE.................................. 37
EXPERIMENT 7: DOES EARTH TURN? 40
EXPERIMENT 8: THE SHIFTING SUN AS SEEN FROM EARTH 44

EXPERIMENT 9: MAPPING THE SUN'S PATH ACROSS THE SKY.......... 48
EXPERIMENT 10: A MODEL TO EXPLAIN EARTH'S SEASONAL
            CHANGES.. 52
EXPERIMENT 11: A MODEL SUNSET AND BLUE SKY 59

CHAPTER 3:
EARTH'S NATURAL SATELLITE: OUR MOON 60

EXPERIMENT 12: THE SIZE OF THE MOON 63
EXPERIMENT 13: THE LIGHT FROM DISTANT SOURCES,
            SUCH AS STARS.. 66
EXPERIMENT 14: WATCHING THE MOON BY DAY AND BY NIGHT 68
EXPERIMENT 15: A MODEL OF MOON, EARTH, AND SUN 73
EXPERIMENT 16: THE MOON'S ORBIT AROUND EARTH AND SUN 78
EXPERIMENT 17: A MODEL OF A LUNAR ECLIPSE 83
EXPERIMENT 18: A MODEL OF A SOLAR ECLIPSE 87

CHAPTER 4:
EARTH'S STAR: THE SUN 92

EXPERIMENT 19: THE DIAMETER OF THE SUN 93

CHAPTER 5:
OTHER PLANETS IN THE SOLAR SYSTEM 96

EXPERIMENT 20: A SCALE MODEL OF THE SOLAR SYSTEM.............. 98

CHAPTER 6:
BEYOND THE SOLAR SYSTEM 102

EXPERIMENT 21: USING PARALLAX TO MEASURE A DISTANCE........ 103
EXPERIMENT 22: A SPECTROSCOPE 110

GLOSSARY 120
FURTHER READING 122
CAREER INFORMATION...................................... 124
INDEX 125

INTRODUCTION

Astronomy is the study of stars and other celestial objects, such as galaxies, planets, moons, asteroids, comets, nebulae, supernovae, gamma ray bursts, and cosmic background microwave radiation. More generally, it involves all phenomena that originate outside Earth's atmosphere. It is among the oldest sciences. Early civilizations—Greek, Indian, Egyptian, and Chinese, among others—carried out methodical observations of the stars and constellations. Do not confuse astronomy with astrology, a pseudoscience based on the belief that human events are correlated with the positions of stars and planets.

Astronomers are scientists who study celestial objects. Astronomers are also known as astrophysicists. They are very well educated and usually have a PhD in physics or astronomy. They are highly intelligent, imaginative, and creative people. They spend most of their time doing research but frequently have additional duties, such as teaching, designing and building instruments, and sharing in the operation of an observatory.

Astronomy deals with extremes. It includes the study of very large things, such as galaxies, and of very small things, such as atoms and subatomic particles. It investigates very hot things like the middle of stars and very cold things like the space between stars and galaxies. To understand these extremes, astronomers have to be famil-

If you are in middle school or high school and know you are interested in becoming an astronomer, you should take physics, chemistry, and all of the math and computer courses offered at your school. Also take courses in English and history that require writing because, as an astronomer, you will have to write reports about your research. Work hard, obtain good grades, and read as much as you can about astronomy as well as the great astronomers who have made outstanding discoveries in the field.

If you do well in these courses, obtain high scores on your SATs, and perform well during college admissions interviews, you will probably be admitted to a university or college where you can major in astronomy, physics, astrophysics, or mathematics. To help gain admission to higher education, you could develop interesting and challenging astronomy projects for science fairs or independent research. These projects will provide useful information for discussion as you meet with college admissions directors.

As you complete high school, try to gain acceptance to the best university or college that your academic record will allow. The better the reputation of a college or university you attend, the better your chances of being accepted for graduate work leading to a PhD in astronomy, astrophysics, or physics.

The path to becoming an astrophysicist or astronomer begins with the pursuit of a four-year bachelor of science degree in astronomy, physics, astrophysics, or mathematics. Once in college, you may be able to major in astronomy. If not, focus on physics and mathematics and take as much astronomy as is offered. Be sure to take computer science courses because computers and computer programming play a major role in present-day astronomy.

During your high school and undergraduate years, make an effort to visit observatories and science museums. Try to meet astronomers and talk with them about their work. Look for opportunities to spend summers working at an observatory or science museum. Your college advisor may be able to help you find such work as a volunteer or as a summer intern or employee.

With a bachelor's degree and solid grades in all your college courses, you will be ready to apply to graduate school. During your junior year of college, make a list of graduate schools you might apply to as a candidate for a PhD in astronomy or astrophysics. Begin to think about which aspect of astronomy you'd like to focus on. Astronomers often specialize in planetary science, solar astronomy, solar origins, solar evolution, or the formation of galaxies.

To be accepted as a PhD candidate, you must do well on the Graduate Record Examination (GRE). Some schools may also require that you take the GRE in physics. If accepted as a candidate for a doctorate in astronomy or physics, plan on spending the next four or five years taking advanced courses, doing research, and writing and defending a dissertation involving original research.

The competition for jobs in astronomy can be intense. When starting out, you may need to look for a postdoctoral position where you can focus on doing research and publishing papers in order to build a reputation. With some experience, you might then seek out a job as an astronomer at a college or university, at a national observatory or national laboratory, or in private industry.

WHAT DO ASTRONOMERS DO?

Once established as an astronomer, your work will probably vary. You may find yourself using a telescope to view stars or galaxies, using a computer to model a theory, conducting research, talking with other astronomers, teaching courses in astronomy, analyzing data, attending meetings or conferences, and writing articles about your research.

For the most part, contemporary spacecraft can reach only celestial objects in or near our solar system within a reasonable time frame. Information about more distant bodies comes from light emitted or reflected by these bodies and collected by telescopes on Earth or on satellites orbiting Earth. Light from celestial objects contains valuable information. The light's intensity reveals the number of photons (light particles) coming from the source. The light's color, both visible and beyond the range of human vision, provides information about the energy of the radiation emitted by the source. Red light has less energy and longer wavelengths than blue light, for example. The visible spectrum constitutes only a small portion of the radiant energy coming from a star or other celestial object. Beyond the range of human vision, astronomers observe ultraviolet light, X-rays, and gamma rays, which are more energetic and have shorter wavelengths than colors in the visible spectrum. They also observe less energetic radiation with longer wavelengths, including infrared radiation, microwaves, and radio waves.

THE SCIENTIFIC METHOD

Most astronomers are involved in scientific research, seeking answers to the problems they strive to understand. They ask questions, make careful observations, and conduct research. Astronomers in different areas of astronomy use different approaches. Depending on the problem, one method is likely to be better than another. Astronomers employ different techniques when they are developing a search for asteroids that might strike Earth, finding the distance to a star, or analyzing the composition of a planet's atmosphere, for instance. Each of these techniques, however, requires an understanding of the scientific method.

In fact, despite the differences, all scientists use this same general approach when reporting their experimental research. In most experiments, scientists perform some or all of the following steps of the scientific method: making an observation, formulating a question, making a hypothesis (one possible answer to the question) and a prediction (an if-then statement), designing and conducting one or more experiments, analyzing the results in order to reach conclusions about the prediction, and accepting or rejecting the hypothesis. Scientists share their findings. They write articles about their experiments and their results. Their writings are then reviewed by other scientists before being published in journals for wider circulation.

You might wonder how to start an experiment. When you observe something in the world, you may become curious and ask a question. Your question, which could arise from an earlier experiment or from reading, may be answered by a well-designed investigation. Once you have a question, you can make a hypothesis. Your hypothesis is a possible answer to your question (what you think will happen). Once you have a hypothesis, it is time to design an experiment to test it.

In most cases, it is appropriate to do a controlled experiment. In a controlled experiment, a scientist forms two groups of subjects that are treated exactly the same—except with regards to the single factor being tested. This factor is called a *variable.*

Two other terms are often used in scientific experiments: *dependent variable* and *independent variable.* A dependent variable depends on the value of independent variables. For example, the area of a plot of land depends on the length and the width of the plot. Here, the dependent variable is the area and the independent variables are the length and the width.

The results of one experiment can lead to a related question. They may send you in an entirely different direction or provide guidance as you dig deeper into the nuances of your problem. Whatever the results, something can be learned from every experiment.

BEFORE YOU BEGIN EXPERIMENTING

As you perform the experiments and other activities in this book, you may need a partner to help you. Work with someone who likes experimenting as much as you do. That way, you will both enjoy what you are doing. **If any safety issues or danger is involved in doing an experiment, you will be warned. In some cases, you will be asked to work with an adult in order to avoid danger. Please do so.** We don't want you to take any chances that could lead to an injury.

Like any good scientist, you will find it useful to record your ideas, notes, data, and conclusions in a notebook. By doing so, you can keep track of the information you gather and the conclusions you reach. These records will help to remind you of what you have learned and may inform your future projects.

SAFETY FIRST

Safety is important in science and engineering. Following certain rules will help to ensure your well-being as you perform your experiments. Some of these rules may seem obvious to you, while others may not—but it is important that you follow all of them.

1. Have an adult help you whenever this book, or any other, so advises.
2. Wear eye protection and closed-toe shoes (not sandals). Tie back long hair.
3. Do not eat or drink while experimenting. Never taste the substances being used (unless instructed to do so).
4. Do not touch chemicals with your bare hands. Use tools, such as spatulas, to transfer chemicals from place to place.
5. Some thermometers contain mercury—a dense liquid metal. It is dangerous to touch mercury or breathe mercury vapor. In fact, mercury thermometers have been banned in many states. When doing experiments that require you to measure temperature, use only electronic or non-mercury thermometers, such as those filled with alcohol. If you have a mercury thermometer in the house, **ask an adult** if it can be taken to a local thermometer exchange location.
6. Do only those experiments that are described in this book or others that have been approved by **an adult**.
7. Maintain a serious attitude when conducting experiments. Never engage in horseplay or play practical jokes.
8. Before beginning an experiment, read all of the instructions carefully and be sure you understand them.
9. Remove any items not needed for the experiment from your work space.

10. At the end of every activity, clean all of the experimental materials and put them away. Then wash your hands thoroughly with soap and water.

The chapters that follow contain experiments relevant to astronomy, along with information that every future young astronomer should know. Hopefully, these resources will help you to decide if astronomy is a field or career path you would like to pursue. Astronomy is vast, and this book's limited space allows for only a brief exploration of the subject. The ideas and experiments introduced here, however, will give you a sense of what interests you might pursue as an astronomer.

CHAPTER ONE

STELLAR CONSTELLATIONS: SHAPES IN THE SKY

Constellations are groups of stars. To early observers, the stars in constellations appeared to form the familiar shapes of things on Earth. In one group of stars, they may have seen an animal or mythological creature, such as a dragon. In another, they saw an object, such as a kite, a coffee pot, or a dish.

Astronomers are familiar with all of the constellations because they use them to indicate the locations of other celestial objects. For example, an astronomer might refer to the nebula in the constellation Orion, allowing other astronomers to locate the nebula via their shared reference point.

Two constellations in the northern sky look like dippers, or ladles. These constellations are actually parts of bigger constellations, technically known as *asterisms.* They can help you find the direction north. In fact, they can lead you to the star Polaris, which is almost directly above Earth's North Pole. Try looking for these constellations in the northern night sky!

THE BIG DIPPER, THE LITTLE DIPPER, AND A DIRECTION

If you live in the United States or Canada, you can see two constellations in the northern sky that look like dippers: the Big Dipper and the Little Dipper. To astronomers, they are parts of the larger constellations Ursa Major and Ursa Minor. On a clear, dark night, you can see them very clearly. Let's take a look.

THINGS YOU WILL NEED

- **an adult**
- **clear night**
- **open area**
- **hammer**
- **2 sticks**

1. Once it is dark, go outside with **an adult**.
2. Find an open area where you can see the northern sky.
3. Look for a group of stars arranged like the ones at the bottom of Figure 1. Those stars form the Big Dipper. The Big Dipper's stars are quite bright. You should be able to find them easily. They may not look exactly like the drawing, however, because the constellation circles around Polaris, the North Star, over the course of each day. To see how the Big Dipper and

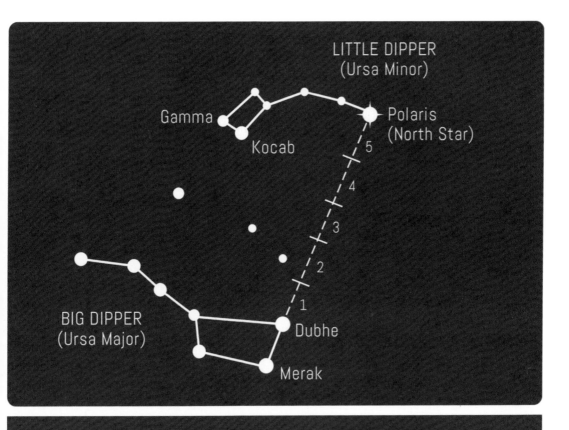

Figure 1. Find the Big Dipper in the northern night sky. Then use it to find Polaris.

Little Dipper may appear as they rotate, slowly turn Figure 1 all the way around.

4. The Little Dipper is not as easy to find. But you can locate it using the pointer stars of the Big Dipper— Merak and Dubhe. While looking at the Big Dipper, extend your arm. Put your first two fingers on the pointer stars, Merak and Dubhe. Keeping your fingers at that distance apart, move them slowly in the

direction given by the pointer stars. The distance from the Big Dipper's pointer stars to the North Star is about five times the distance between your fingers. So, keeping your fingers that distance apart, move your two fingers five times along the direction given by the pointer stars. You will arrive at the North Star. The North Star, or Polaris, is at the end of the handle of the Little Dipper.

Polaris is not a bright star. It's about as bright as Merak. Follow the Little Dipper's handle to the dipper itself. Depending on their orientations at a given time, the Little Dipper may appear be pouring water into the Big Dipper, or vice versa.

In addition to forming part of the handle of the Little Dipper, the North Star also resides almost directly above Earth's North Pole, providing a handy way to tell directions.

5. Now that you have located Polaris, have a partner stand a few meters or yards away from you, under your sightline to the star.

6. Drive a stake into the ground where you are standing. Drive a second stake into the ground where your partner is standing. The line formed between the two stakes should point more or less in the direction of the North Pole—north.

EXPERIMENT 2

CAN A MAGNETIC COMPASS BE USED TO FIND TRUE NORTH?

Many people think that a magnetic compass needle always points toward the North Pole. In this experiment, you'll see if that is true.

THINGS YOU WILL NEED

- **magnetic compass**
- **the north-pointing line you made in Experiment 1**

1. Find the north-pointing line you made in Experiment 1, and stand above the first stake.
2. Hold a magnetic compass above the line. Is the compass needle parallel to the north-pointing line on the ground? You will probably find that it is not. Unless you live on a line extending from Florida's panhandle to Lake Superior's western shore, the compass will not point as accurately toward true north as Polaris does.

TRUE NORTH: AN EXPLANATION

The line you marked in Experiment 1 should point in a direction that is very close to true north. Polaris is less than one degree away from a point directly over the North Pole.

A compass needle, on the other hand, does not point toward Earth's North Pole. It points instead toward Earth's magnetic North Pole. This magnetic pole is located in Canada in the Boothia Peninsula. It is about 1,900 kilometers (1,200 miles) from Earth's geographic North Pole. Unlike the geographic North Pole, the magnetic North Pole is not fixed, but moves.

If you live in the eastern United States, your compass needle will probably point west of true north. In the western United States, compass needles point east of true north.

EXPERIMENT 3

FINDING THE NORTH POLAR CONSTELLATIONS

The north polar constellations are a group of constellations that surround Polaris and are located directly above an area north of the Arctic Circle, 66.5 degrees north of the North Pole. See if you can find and identify the north polar constellations. Figure 2 may help you.

THINGS YOU WILL NEED

- **clear night**

Many constellations are only visible at certain times of the year, but the north polar constellations can be seen every night. Can you explain why?

1. Figure 2 will help you to identify the major constellations surrounding Polaris. Can you find all of them?
2. Many think Cassiopeia looks like a dentist's chair. Some see Cepheus as a kite. Draco is often called a dragon or a kite with a long tail. What do they look like to you?

   Do you think the north polar constellations always look the same, or do their positions change?

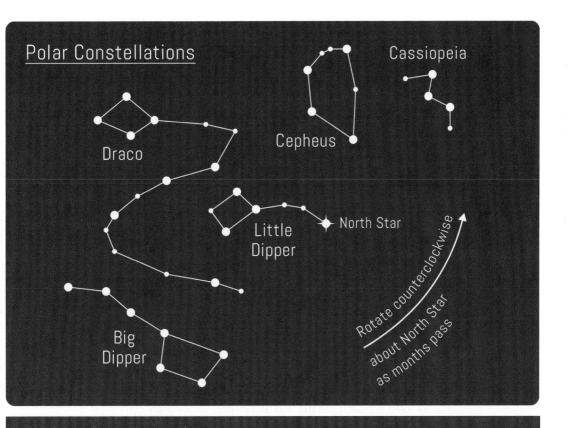

Figure 2. The north polar constellations turn about the North Star.

EXPERIMENT 4

LOCATING THE NORTH POLAR CONSTELLATIONS OVER TIME IN HOURS

THINGS YOU WILL NEED

- **clear sky**
- **good visibility**
- **alarm clock**
- **notebook and pencil**

During Experiment 3, you found and identified the north polar constellations. If you live in the southern part of the United States, some parts of the north polar constellations are not visible all the time. Further south, at the equator, Polaris sits on the horizon, so some of the north polar constellations are never visible.

Do you think the positions of the north polar constellations will appear to turn during the night hours? Here's how you can find out.

1. Observe the north polar constellations, especially the Big Dipper and Cassiopeia, soon after dark. Make a drawing of their appearance in the sky.
2. With parental permission, set your alarm clock for an early morning hour before dawn. Get up and observe the constellations again. What do you find? Have their positions changed? If so, how did they change?

EXPERIMENT 5

OBSERVING THE NORTH POLAR CONSTELLATIONS OVER TIME IN MONTHS

If you go to bed early, ask permission to stay up later on a clear night at least once a month. This way, you'll be able to observe the constellations and see if they change positions as the months pass.

THINGS YOU WILL NEED

- **clear sky**
- **good visibility**
- **notebook and pencil**

1. Draw a picture of the Big Dipper as you see it, recording the date and time.
2. Make new drawings of the position of the Big Dipper at the same hour of the day about a month later.
3. Repeat this procedure again each month for the next few months.

    What can you conclude?

FINDING AND WATCHING THE NORTH POLAR CONSTELLATIONS: AN EXPLANATION

In Experiment 4, you saw that the north polar constellations change their positions in the sky over the course of a night. From your perspective, standing on Earth, they seem to turn slowly in a counterclockwise direction around Polaris.

These constellations only appear to move, however, because Earth is turning on its axis, rotating 360 degrees each day. As a result, the constellations, which do not move, appear to turn 360 degrees every twenty-four hours—in the direction opposite Earth's rotation.

In addition to rotating on its axis, Earth also makes one orbit around the sun every 365.25 days. As Earth moves along its orbit, the view of the sky and stars changes. In fact, if you look, you will see a slightly different sky each succeeding night.

Figure 3 shows what the Big Dipper looks like at 9 p.m. in the middle of each month, over the course of an entire year. You must have found something similar during your investigation.

Notice that the line connecting the pointer stars moves like a clock hand that turns backward. In January, the line is at three o'clock. In February, the line is at two o'clock. In March, it's at one o'clock, and so on. Along with this line, all of the constellations appear to move counterclockwise during the year. This is because Earth moves around the sun in the opposite direction, providing a shifting view.

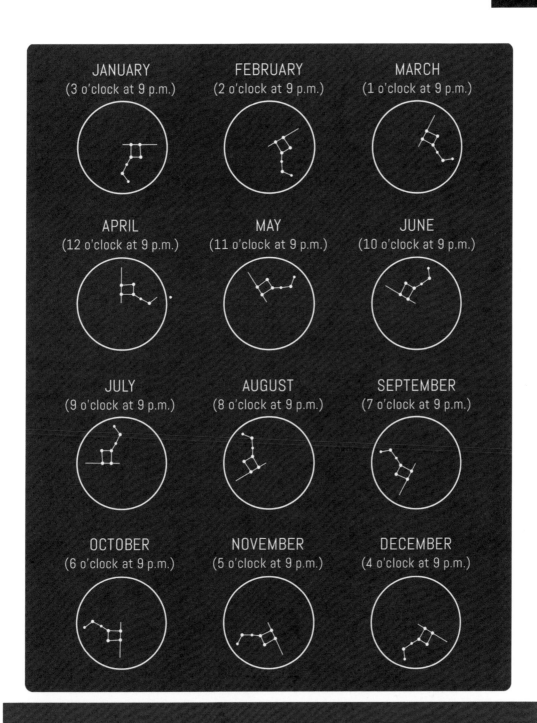

Figure 3. The Big Dipper seen monthly at about 9 p.m.

In reality, the stars themselves move very little. It is now common knowledge that the illusion of their motion actually reflects the motion of Earth; it is Earth that moves. Ancient astronomers, however, believed that Earth was the center of the universe and that the stars, including Earth's sun, revolved around it.

Because Earth revolves around the sun, the sky visible to the planet's inhabitants changes a little bit each night. The stars and constellations in the night sky change slowly from month to month as Earth completes its orbit. See Figure 4.

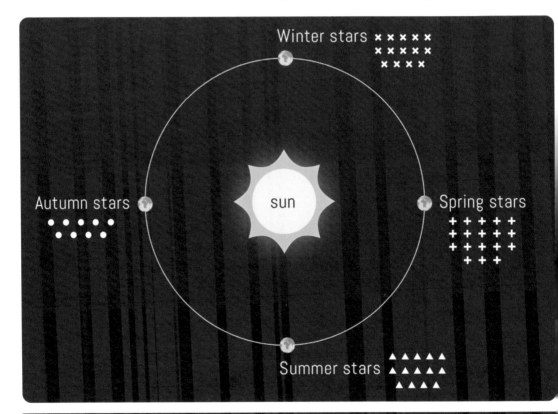

Figure 4. As seasons change on Earth, so do the stars seen in the night sky.

CONSTELLATIONS TO WATCH EACH SEASON

You can't see all of the constellations at the same time. The set of constellations you can see changes from season to season as Earth moves along its orbit. Figure 5 shows some of the major constellations visible during autumn.

AUTUMN

As the Big Dipper sinks toward the northern horizon and Cassiopeia moves ever higher in the sky, Pegasus can be seen high in the southern sky. It looks like a square with handles. Cygnus, high in the western sky, is called the Northern Cross because of its shape. Deneb, a bright star, can be found at the top of the cross. Other constellations visible in the autumn sky include Auriga—with its bright alpha star, Capella—to the east and Cepheus and Cassiopeia to the north.

WINTER

The constellation Orion, with its bright three-star belt, is easily found high in the winter sky (Figure 6). During the evening in December and January, you can see Orion by looking up high in the southeast. Once you see it, you'll never forget it. Slightly to the southeast of Orion, you'll see Canis Major (the greater dog), which contains Sirius, the brightest star in the sky. Also above Orion, the constellation of Taurus (the Bull) appears, containing the bright star Aldebaran. Additionally, you may spy the small but beautiful Pleiades, which looks like a small dipper. Northeast of Orion, you can see the constellation Gemini— meaning "twins" in Latin. The brightest two stars in Gemini are its twin stars, Castor and Pollux.

You'll be able to watch Orion through the winter and into the spring. In which direction does it seem to move as the weeks and months pass?

SPRING

In the early spring, Orion is still visible in the southwest in the early evening (Figure 7). The constellation Bootes can be seen quite high in the eastern or southeastern sky. It has the shape of a warped kite and contains the bright star Arcturus. Virgo, which has a dish shape, is southwest of Bootes. Cepheus and Cassiopeia are north of Bootes. What other constellations can you identify in the spring sky?

SUMMER

The coffee pot shape of Sagittarius (Figure 8) is easy to find in the southern sky during the summer. To the northeast of Sagittarius, you will find Cygnus, and further north, you'll again find the north polar constellations Cepheus and Cassiopeia. West of Sagittarius, you may find Scorpius, including its bright star, Antares. Further west lies Virgo with its brightest star, Spica.

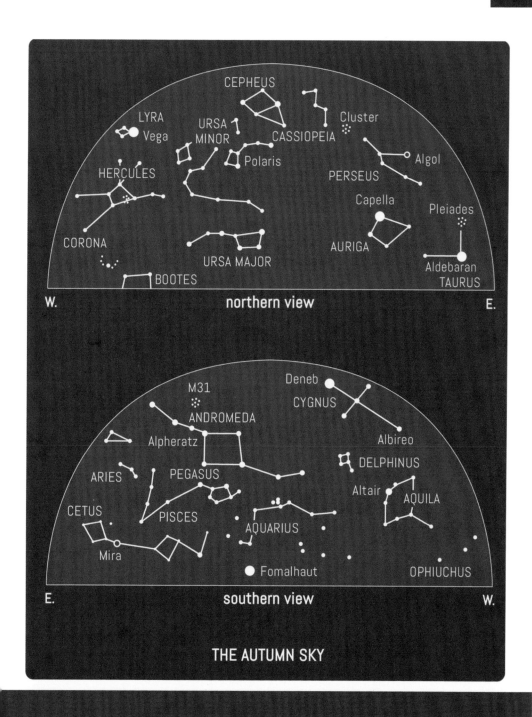

Figure 5. The autumn sky

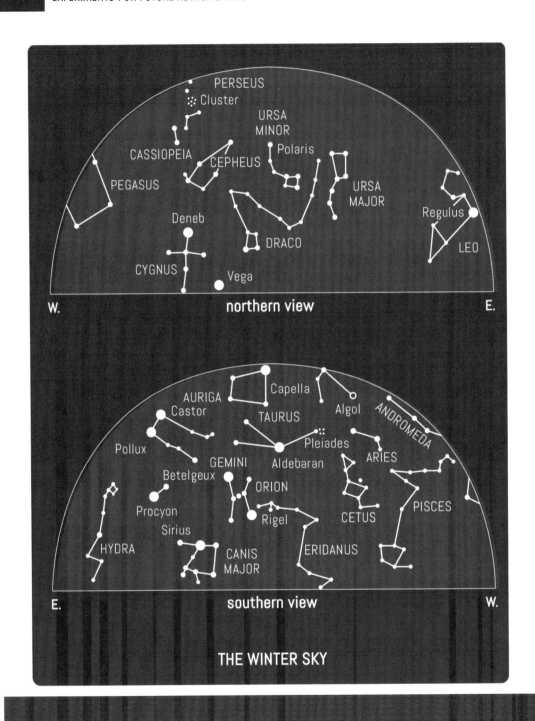

Figure 6. The winter sky

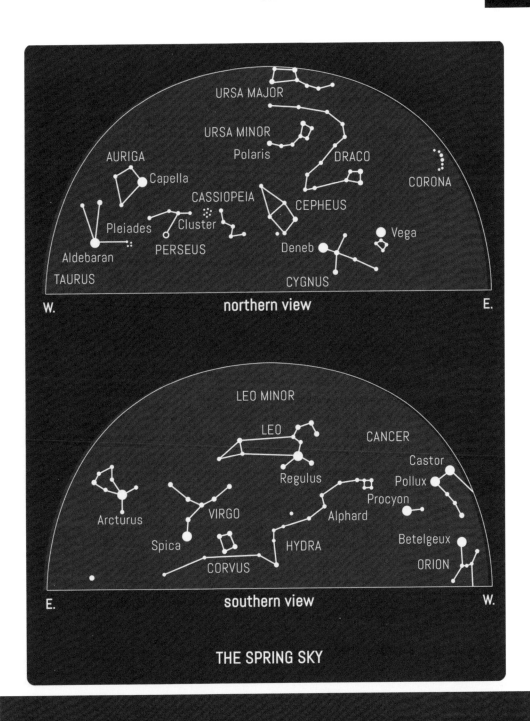

Figure 7. The spring sky

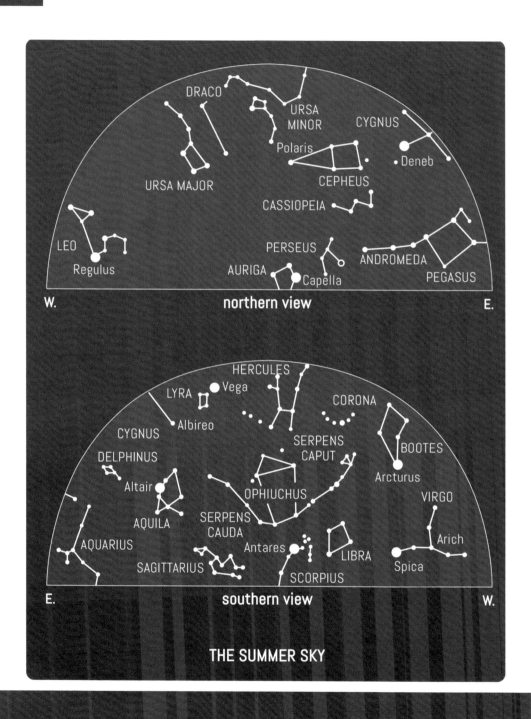

Figure 8. The summer sky

CHAPTER TWO

EARTH: ONE OF THE SUN'S SATELLITES

Earth, your home in the solar system, is the third planet from the sun. It is the only planet where scientists can be certain that life exists. Over time, scientists and geographers have mapped the planet, establishing lines of latitude and longitude as a means of understanding the relationships between different locations on the globe.

Figure 9 shows how Earth is divided into these imaginary lines of latitude and longitude. Greenwich, England, was established as the point of zero-degree (0°) longitude. Lines of longitude extend from 0 to 180 degrees east and west of Greenwich. The equator was established as the line of 0-degree latitude, with lines of latitude extending from 0 to 90 degrees to the north and south.

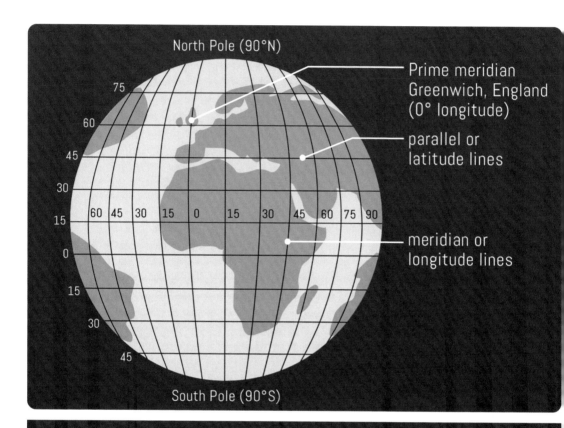

North Pole (90°N)

75

60

45

30

15

0

15

30

45

60 45 30 15 0 15 30 45 60 75 90

Prime meridian
Greenwich, England
(0° longitude)

parallel or
latitude lines

meridian or
longitude lines

South Pole (90°S)

Figure 9. Geographers use an imaginary grid over the globe to pinpoint locations. The lines of longitude are known as *meridians* and run between north and south, marking points between east and west. Lines of latitude are known as *parallels* and run between east and west, marking points between north and south. Philadelphia is approximately 75 degrees west of Greenwich, England, and 40 degrees north of the equator. Can you find it on a globe?

EXPERIMENT 6

YOUR LATITUDE

Do you know the latitude where you live? You can make a pretty good estimate of your latitude by measuring the altitude of the North Star, Polaris, which is located almost directly above Earth's North Pole.

As you can see from Figure 10, the altitude—the angle of elevation above the horizon—of Polaris is equal to the latitude from which its altitude is measured. Because Polaris is so far from Earth, light rays coming from the star are parallel.

THINGS YOU WILL NEED

- **square piece of cardboard about 12 in (30 cm) on a side**
- **large protractor**
- **wide soda straw**
- **string**
- **paper clip**
- **nail to punch hole through cardboard**
- **washer**
- **tape**
- **a partner (optional)**

1. To find Polaris, go back to Experiment 1. Find the Big Dipper and use the pointer stars, Dubhe and Merak, to form a line that points toward Polaris. The distance of Polaris from the Big Dipper is about five times the distance between these two pointer stars.

2. To measure the altitude of Polaris, you can build an astrolabe. See Figure 11 and use it to construct your astrolabe.

3. When you look at the North Star through the soda straw, the string will hang along a line that measures the star's altitude. What is the altitude of Polaris? What is the latitude of your location? (It may help to have a partner to help mark where the string hangs.)

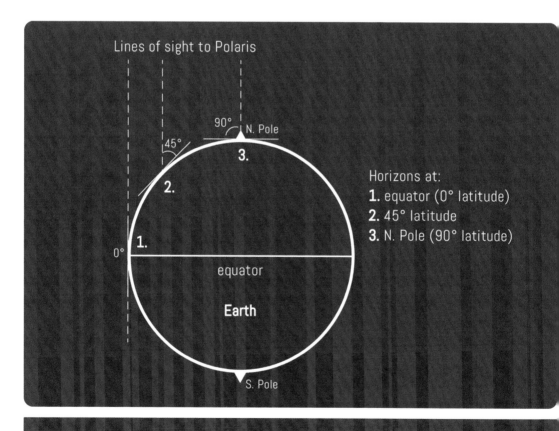

Figure 10. You can find your latitude by measuring the altitude of Polaris.

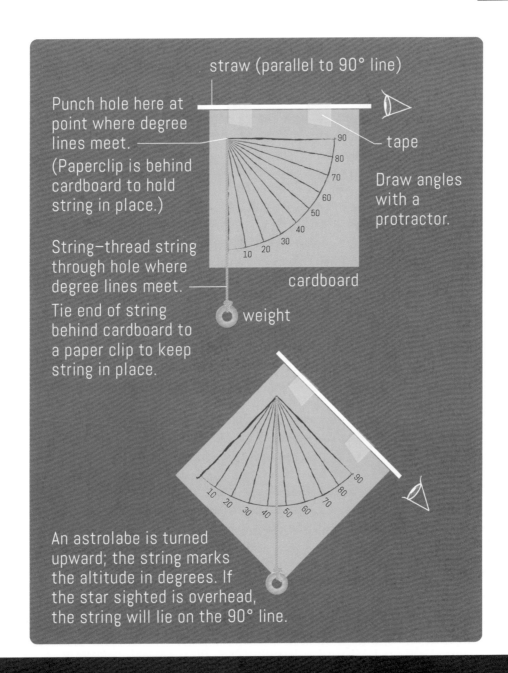

straw (parallel to 90° line)

Punch hole here at point where degree lines meet. — (Paperclip is behind cardboard to hold string in place.)

90
80
70
60
50
40
30
20
10

tape

Draw angles with a protractor.

String–thread string through hole where degree lines meet. —

cardboard

Tie end of string behind cardboard to a paper clip to keep string in place.

weight

10 20 30 40 50 60 70 80 90

An astrolabe is turned upward; the string marks the altitude in degrees. If the star sighted is overhead, the string will lie on the 90° line.

Figure 11. You can build an astrolabe to measure the altitude of stars, planets, and the moon.

EXPERIMENT 7

DOES EARTH TURN?

The sun appears to move around Earth at a rate of 15 degrees per hour. As you probably know, the sun itself does not actually move. It is Earth that rotates from west to east, making the sun appear to move from east to west. Since the time of Galileo, astronomers have been certain of this reality—that even though the sun, moon, and stars appear to move around Earth, it is actually Earth that turns. But how can they be certain? In truth, there was no direct proof until 1851, when Jean Foucault, a French physicist, carried out an experiment to show that Earth rotates.

Foucault hung a 65-meter-long (213 ft) pendulum with a 28-kilogram (62 lb) bob from the dome of the Pantheon in Paris. He knew that a pendulum maintained the plane of its swing. If Earth was turning, then, he reasoned, the plane of the pendulum's swing would appear to move westward as Earth rotated beneath it.

Some science museums have Foucault pendulums. If you go to such a museum, you can see for yourself that Earth really does rotate.

You can make a simple model to show how a Foucault pendulum works.

1. Make a pendulum from a heavy metal washer and a piece of thread.
2. Use tape to hang the pendulum from a cabinet or table as shown in Figure 12.

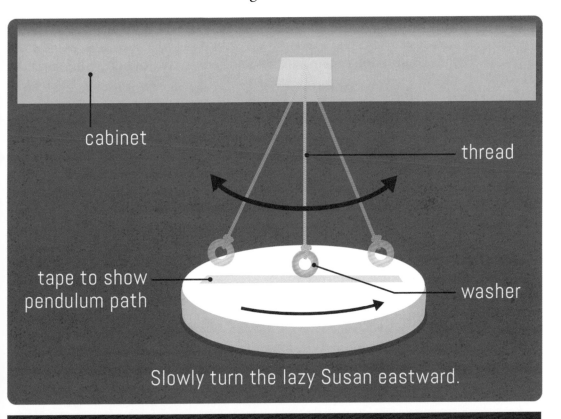

cabinet

thread

tape to show
pendulum path

washer

Slowly turn the lazy Susan eastward.

Figure 12. In this model of a Foucault pendulum, the center of the lazy Susan represents Earth's North Pole. What happens to the apparent path of the pendulum as "Earth" turns from west to east?

3. Set the pendulum swinging above a lazy Susan. The center of the lazy Susan represents Earth's North Pole.
4. Use pieces of tape to show the plane of the pendulum's swing.
5. Slowly turn the lazy Susan from west to east to represent a rotating Earth. Notice how the plane of the pendulum's swing appears to rotate from east to west—just as Foucault's pendulum did in the Pantheon.

EARTH AND THE NEARBY SKY

If you step outside on a clear day and look upward, you will see the blue dome commonly known as the *sky*. **Never look directly at the sun; it can cause permanent damage to your eyes**. In the sky—or celestial hemisphere, as an astronomer would say—you will likely see the sun, perhaps the moon, and if you look very carefully, the planet Venus. At night, you will often see the moon, thousands of stars, and even one or more planets. To most people, the stars seem to be scattered randomly across the sky, but others see them as forming definite patterns.

The sun, appearing from Earth to be the brightest of all the stars, rises and sets daily, creating the experience of day and night. There are two possible explanations for the sun's apparent motion. One is that the sun makes a circular path around Earth each day. The other is that Earth turns on its axis each day, making the sun appear to move around Earth.

Based on what you know about Foucault's experiment, you're probably convinced that the second explanation is the correct one.

WHERE ARE WE?

Positions on Earth can be identified by using a giant imaginary grid that covers the planet's surface. These are the lines you see on maps and globes. The lines that run north-south are called *meridians* and measure longitude. The prime meridian is the line marking zero-degree longitude. It runs from pole to pole through Greenwich, England. If you look on a globe, you will see that the distance between these longitude lines is greatest at the equator, and that the lines join to form a point at each pole.

The sun seems to move in a circle around Earth once every twenty-four hours. Since there are 360 degrees in a circle, the sun moves 15 degrees of longitude every hour. That's why time zones are about 15 degrees apart. When you move westward from one time zone to the next, you set your clock back one hour. Why aren't all time zones exactly 15 degrees apart?

Imaginary lines parallel to the equator are called *parallels*. They are used to measure latitude—degrees north or south of the equator. Degrees of latitude are about 111 kilometers (69 miles) apart. The North Pole is at 90 degrees latitude; the equator is 0 degrees latitude; and this book was written at 42 degrees latitude.

EXPERIMENT 8

THE SHIFTING SUN AS SEEN FROM EARTH

THINGS YOU WILL NEED

- **hand drill**
- **pliers**
- **square board about 12 in (30 cm) on a side**
- **new, unsharpened pencil, broken or sawed in half**
- **white paper**
- **ruler**

The sun does not follow the same path across the sky each day. The summer sun follows a longer and higher path than the winter sun does. To find the path of the sun at various times of the year, you can build a sundial.

1. Use the hand drill to make a hole in the board— with the same diameter as the pencil. The hole should be near the center of one side of the board and about 1 cm (2 to 3 inches) in from the side. Use Figure 13a as a reference.
2. Insert the end of the pencil into the hole in the board. If the pencil is loose, use some clay to support it. The pencil should rise about 10 to 13 cm (4 to 5 inches) above the surface of the board.
3. Place the sundial on a level surface along a north-south line like the one you established in Experiment 1.

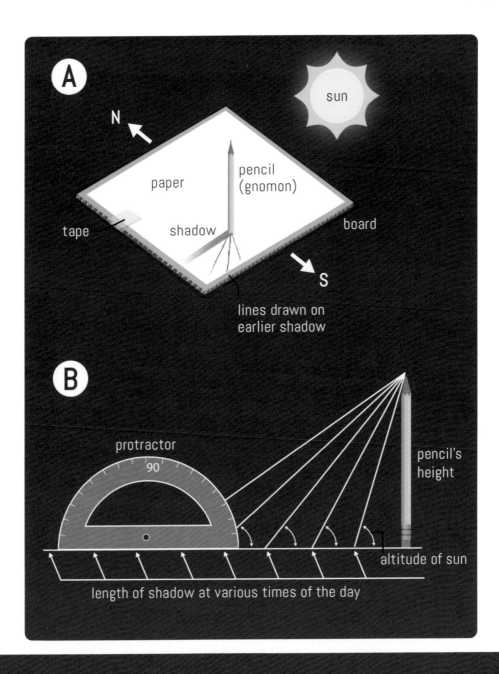

Figure 13. a) You can make a sundial. b) Use the lengths of the sundial pencil's shadows to determine the sun's altitude at different times.

4. The pencil, which forms the gnomon of the sundial, should be near the south end of the board. Use a small carpenter's level to be certain that the board is level and that the pencil is perpendicular to its surface.

5. Cover the board with a sheet of white paper or brown wrapping paper.

6. Cut a slit along the south edge of the paper so that it will fit around the pencil.

7. Tape the paper to the board. You are now ready to make measurements.

8. Early in the morning, when the sun begins to cast shadows of the pencil onto the paper, begin making measurements. With a ruler, draw a line along the center of the shadow from the pencil to the end of the shadow. (If the shadow extends beyond the board, place another board beside your sundial and measure the total length of the shadow.) Measure the shadow from the base of the pencil to the end of the shadow. Write the length of the shadow and the time you made the measurement along the line you have drawn.

9. Repeat this procedure at frequent intervals throughout the day.

10. To establish a north-south line on your sundial, take frequent measurements of the pencil's shadow around midday. The shortest shadow cast by the pencil will occur when the sun is due south. At that time, the pencil's shadow will lie along a north-south line.

11. At sunset, you can bring the paper inside.

12. To determine the sun's position in the sky at various times during the day, draw a north-south line through the shortest shadow. Draw an east-west line perpendicular to the north-south line. The sun's azimuth is its angle along the horizon relative to north. North is 0 degrees, east is 90 degrees, south is at 180 degrees, and west is 270 degrees. With a protractor, determine the sun's azimuth for each of the shadow-lines you drew.

13. The sun's altitude is its angle above the horizon. If the sun is on the horizon, its altitude is 0 degrees. If it is directly overhead, it is 90 degrees. To determine the sun's altitude at each of the times you measured it, draw a vertical line equal to the height of the pencil. At the base of this line, draw a line equal to the length of the pencil's longest shadow. (This line should make a right angle with the line representing the height of the pencil.) Mark the length of the shadow for each of the times you measured it on this line. A line connecting the shadow's length and the pencil's height will enable you to find the sun's altitude for each of the times you marked the sun's shadow. Use a protractor to measure the angle as shown in Figure 13b.

   With the information you have, you could map the sun's position in the sky at each of the times you took a measurement with the sundial. An easier way is to map its path by using a marking pen on a clear dome (see Experiment 9).

EXPERIMENT 9

MAPPING THE SUN'S PATH ACROSS THE SKY

THINGS YOU WILL NEED

- **clear plastic dome or fine-mesh kitchen strainer**
- **cardboard**
- **pencil**
- **ruler**
- **tape**
- **sunny, level surface**
- **marking pen or round-headed pins or small pieces of masking tape**
- **calendar**

During the course of a day, the sun seems to move from east to west, but what path does it take across the sky? You can map the sun's path by using a clear plastic dome or a fine-mesh kitchen strainer to represent the sky. Astronomers call the sky the *celestial hemisphere.* If you think about it, the sky does resemble a "half-sphere"—the literal meaning of *hemisphere.* This is because you see only half the sky at any one time. The other half is blocked out by the earth. Twelve hours later, you can see the other half of the sky. The total sky—the sky surrounding the entire globe—is called the *celestial sphere.*

1. To map the sun's path across the celestial hemisphere, place the dome or strainer on a sheet of cardboard.

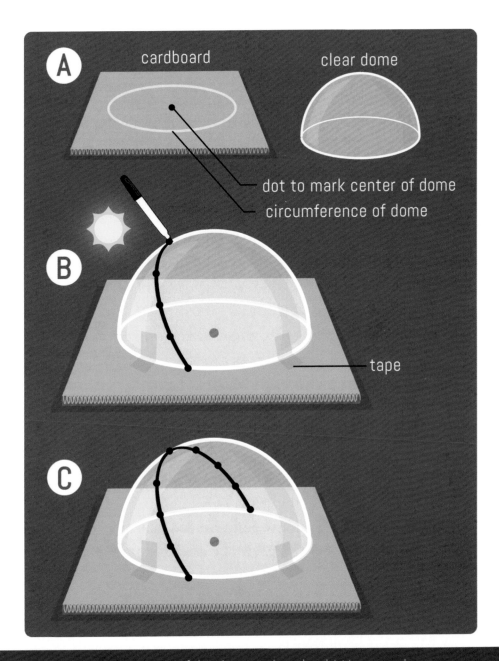

Inside the figure:

A   cardboard   clear dome

dot to mark center of dome

circumference of dome

B   tape

C

Figure 14. a) Mark the center of the dome with a dot. b) Use a marking pen to map the sun's position in the sky. The shadow of the pen's tip should fall on the dot at the center of the dome. c) By the end of the day, you will have a map of the sun's path across the sky.

2. Use a pencil to mark the edge of the dome or strainer on the cardboard as shown in Figure 14a.

3. Remove the dome or strainer. Use a ruler and the pencil to make a dot at the center of the circle you drew on the cardboard.

4. Put the dome or strainer back in its original position and tape it to the cardboard.

5. Shortly after sunrise, place the dome or strainer outside on a level surface that will be bathed in sunlight all day. Mark the position of the cardboard so that you can put it back in the same place if it should be moved accidentally.

6. If you are using a clear plastic dome, you can mark the sun's path across the sky with a marking pen. Place the tip of the pen on the dome so that its shadow falls on the dot you drew at the center of the dome (Figure 14b). Mark that point on the dome. That point on the dome corresponds to the sun's place in the celestial hemisphere. The dot represents your position at the center of the celestial hemisphere. (If you use a strainer, round-headed pins or small pieces of masking tape can be used to cast shadows on the dot.)

7. Continue to mark the sun's position on the dome or strainer as often as you can throughout the day. Together, all the marks, pins, or pieces of tape will make a map of the sun's path across the sky. (See Figure 14c.) If you used a strainer, connect the pins

or pieces of tape with a piece of colored yarn so that you will have a permanent map of the sun's path.

8. Repeat this experiment at different times of the year. If possible, try to map the sun on or about the twentieth of June, September, December, and March. Differently colored marks can be used to identify the date of each experiment if you have only one dome.

These maps of the sun's path will help you to confirm or answer a number of questions. For example, does the sun rise and set in the same place every day? Does the sun's path across the sky change over the course of a year? Does the sun's midday altitude change? When is the sun's path across the sky longest? Shortest? Does the sun always rise at an azimuth of 90 degrees and set at 270 degrees? When does the sun reach its greatest altitude? How might you use your maps to determine the answers to these questions?

EXPERIMENT 10

A MODEL TO EXPLAIN EARTH'S SEASONAL CHANGES

THINGS YOU WILL NEED

- **bright lightbulb**
- **table**
- **dark room**
- **small globe or a ball**
- **cardboard mailing tube**
- **flashlight**
- **sheet of white paper**
- **partner**
- **pencil**

You know that the sun's path across the sky changes from season to season. To explain Earth's seasonal changes, you need to know that Earth's axis is tilted at 23.5 degrees to its orbit about the sun (Figure 15a). You can make a model to explain Earth's seasons.

1. To see how the tilt of Earth's axis affects the angle of sunlight, place a bright lightbulb in the center of a table in a dark room. Then move a small globe or ball in a large circle around the bulb to represent the movement of Earth around the sun. Keep the globe or ball tipped at about a 23-degree angle (see Figure 15a) as you move it along its circular path.

2. Stop at point S (summer) and turn the globe or ball to represent Earth's rotation on its axis. Which part of

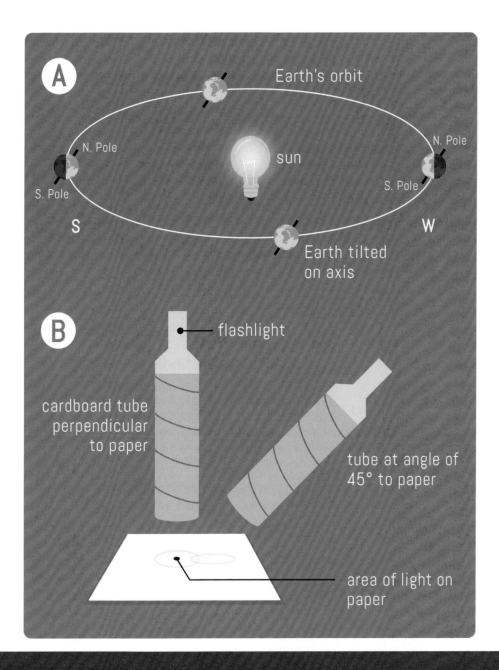

Figure 15. a) Earth's axis is tilted 23.5 degrees. This tilt creates seasons (summer, S, and winter, W) as Earth orbits the sun. b) The angle at which sunlight strikes Earth affects the temperature of the area it strikes.

the globe remains lit throughout the rotation? At the peak of summer, the sun never sets on this part of the planet. Which part of the planet is this? Which part of the globe remains dark throughout the rotation—indicating that the sun never rises?

3. Repeat this process at point W (winter).

4. To see how the angle at which light strikes Earth affects a season's average temperature, tape a long section of a cardboard mailing tube to the end of a flashlight. (See Figure 15b.)

5. Place the end of the tube several inches (10–25 cm) above and perpendicular to a white sheet of paper, as shown. Have a partner use a pencil to mark an outline of the light that falls on the paper. Keeping the tube the same distance from the paper, tilt the flashlight and tube so that the light falls on the paper at a greater angle. Again, have someone mark the outline of the light on the paper. Continue changing the angle of the tube until the tube is almost parallel to the paper.

The amount of light coming through the tube is constant, just as light emitted by the sun is constant. But what happens to the area of the light on the paper as the tube moves from a position perpendicular to the paper to one that is nearly parallel? Which condition is closest to summertime? To wintertime? How is the area over which the light energy spreads related to the season's average temperature?

THE EARTH IS A SPHERE

People have known for centuries that Earth is a sphere, but the spectacular views from satellites, and especially from the moon, should finally convince even members of the Flat Earth Society.

Early evidence about the shape of Earth was subtler. For example, during an eclipse of the moon, Earth's shadow appears to be curved as it crosses the moon. As early as the fourth century BCE, Eratosthenes estimated the radius of Earth. He knew that on the first day of summer, the sun was directly overhead in the city of Syene—now Aswan. He knew this because the image of the sun could be seen reflected in the water of a deep well in Syene on that day. Eratosthenes lived in Alexandria, which was 500 miles (804.67 km) north of Syene. At noon on the first day of summer, when he knew the sun was directly overhead in Syene, he measured the shadow of a tall pillar in Alexandria. He found that the sun's rays made an angle of 7.5 degrees with the pillar.

Knowing the sun's rays were parallel, he reasoned that 500 miles (804.67 km) would be equivalent to 7.5 degrees of the 360 degrees along Earth's circumference (Figure 16). Each 1,000 miles (1,609.34 km), then, would be equivalent to 15 degrees. Dividing 360 degrees by 15, he found 24 and concluded that the entire circumference of Earth must be 24,000 miles (38,624.26 km). Its diameter, then, is 24,000 miles divided by pi (π). The diameter of any circle

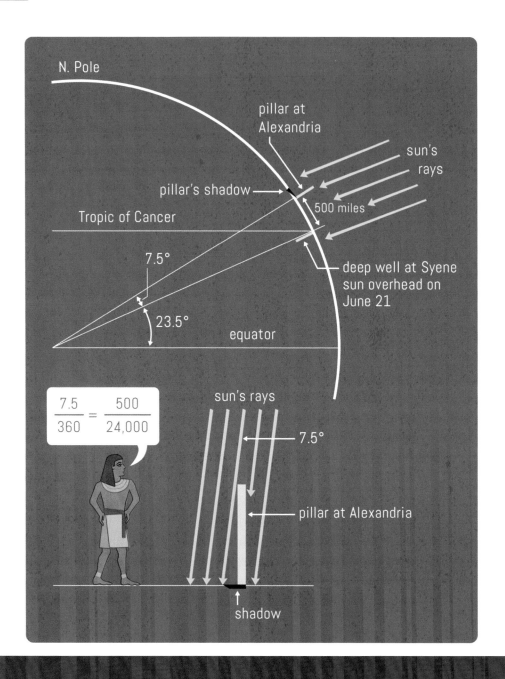

Figure 16. Eratosthenes first calculated Earth's circumference.

can be calculated by dividing its circumference by pi, a number equal to approximately 3.14. Hence, Eratosthenes determined that Earth's diameter was about 8,000 miles (12,874.75 km), and that its radius was 4,000 miles (6,437.38 km).

Early sailors knew that the altitude of the North Star decreased as they sailed south. Once they sailed south of the equator, Polaris dropped below the horizon. Such observations can be explained by the fact that Earth is a sphere. In fact, as you saw from Figure 10, the altitude of the North Star is equal to the latitude from which it is viewed.

By the eighteenth century, educated people believed that the sun, the moon, and the stars appeared to move across the sky because Earth rotated on its axis once each day. But direct evidence of Earth's rotation was not available before the middle of the nineteenth century, when Jean Foucault built his famous pendulum (see Experiment 7).

Because a pendulum will maintain its direction of swing, Foucault knew that Earth must be rotating when he saw the pendulum slowly change its path.

BLUE SKIES AND RED SUNSETS

Sometime during your life, you have likely wondered why the sky is blue. If you didn't get a satisfactory answer then, we will give it to you now. The sky is blue because of the composition of Earth's atmosphere. The oxygen and nitrogen molecules and other particles in the atmosphere absorb and emit light—a process called *scattering*. Because these gases tend to scatter the shorter wavelengths of light (blue) more than longer wavelengths (red), and because the scattered light is emitted in all directions, the sky appears blue. In space, where there is no atmosphere, light is not scattered. As a result, we can see light coming from stars, but the space around the stars appears black because there is nothing in the vacuum of space to scatter light.

On Earth, as the sun approaches the horizon, its light must travel through a greater length of atmosphere. Because sunlight encounters more and more gas as it sinks toward the horizon, more and more of the light at the blue end of the spectrum is scattered. Red light is scattered the least. Hence, the setting sun appears redder and redder as it approaches the horizon because only reddish light from the sun comes all the way through the atmosphere.

You can make a model sunset to see the blue "sky" caused by scattered light, along with a red "sunset."

EXPERIMENT 11

A MODEL SUNSET AND BLUE SKY

1. In a dark room, shine the light from a slide projector or other light source through a fish tank full of water.

2. To scatter light, add a small amount of powdered milk or a nondairy creamer to the water and stir. Notice how the light coming through the water begins to take on a bluish color as it is scattered by the milky particles.

3. Continue adding small amounts of the powder and stirring. What happens to the color of the light emerging from the water at the end of the tank? Can you see a "setting sun"?

THINGS YOU WILL NEED

- **dark room**
- **slide projector or equivalent light source**
- **fish tank**
- **water**
- **powdered milk or nondairy creamer**
- **big spoon for stirring**

CHAPTER THREE

EARTH'S NATURAL SATELLITE: OUR MOON

Objects that orbit, or move around a planet, are called satellites. There are many satellites orbiting Earth. All but one of them have been placed in orbit by rockets that launched them into space from Earth. Earth's only natural satellite is the moon. Some planets, such as Jupiter, have many moons. Earth has only one.

Each day, the sun rises in the east and sets in the west. The sun's motion is only apparent because Earth makes one full turn on its axis once every twenty-four hours; Earth is a satellite of the sun. Earth, too, has its own natural satellite—the moon. The moon is less consistent. It rises and sets at different times, and its shape changes from day to day and from night to night.

In this chapter, you will investigate the moon by watching how it changes with time. You may be surprised to learn that you can often see the moon during the day as well as at night. There are also days when you can't see the moon at any time. You will investigate the moon's path around Earth and the sun, and you will make models to demonstrate what happens when Earth passes between the moon and the sun, or when the moon passes between Earth and the sun.

DISTANCE TO THE MOON BY LASER BEAM

Today, it's easy to measure the distance to the moon because astronauts left a reflector on the moon. The time it takes for a laser pulse to reach the moon and be reflected back to Earth can be measured—as approximately 2.6 seconds. A laser pulse travels at the speed of light (300,000 km/s). The distance the laser light travels—twice the distance to the moon—can then be calculated: 2.6 s x 300,000 km/s = 750,000 km. The distance to the moon is therefore half that distance: 750,000 km/2 = 375,000 km or 233,000 miles. This distance varies, however, because the moon's orbit is elliptical.

This task was not as easy for ancient astronomers, but they were able to make reasonable estimates of the moon's distance using the geometry they had invented.

MEASURING THE DISTANCE TO THE MOON

Early astronomers estimated the distance to the moon in several ways. Figure 17 shows one of these methods.

Two astronomers observed the moon at a considerable, but known, distance apart on Earth's surface. Each had agreed to focus on a particular point (P) on the moon at the same

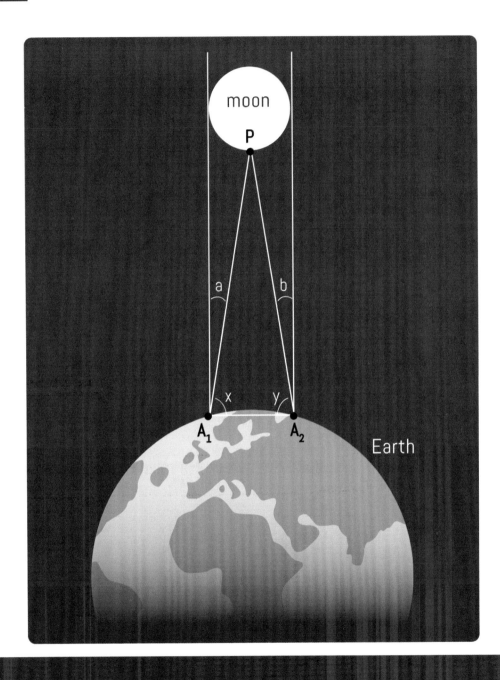

Figure 17. Early scientists measured the distance to the moon using their knowledge of geometry and a distant star.

time. Each measured the angle between their lines of sight to that point and their lines of sight to a distant star. They knew that their sightlines to the star would be parallel—because light rays from a distant source are always parallel, as you will see in the next experiment (Experiment 12).

One astronomer measured angles *a* and *x*; the other measured angles *b* and *y*. With that information, and the measured distance between them, they could construct the triangle A_1A_2P. (It was a much longer and skinnier triangle than the one in the drawing.) Their experimental results indicated that the distance to the moon was approximately sixty Earth radii or 386,000 km (240,000 miles).

EXPERIMENT

THE SIZE OF THE MOON

Knowing the distance to the moon makes it easy to find its size.

1. Use a pencil and a ruler to draw a square 0.25 inch (0.6 cm) long and wide near the center of a file card.

THINGS YOU WILL NEED

- **pencil**
- **ruler**
- **file card**
- **scissors**
- **yardstick or meterstick**
- **clay**
- **moon with full diameter visible**

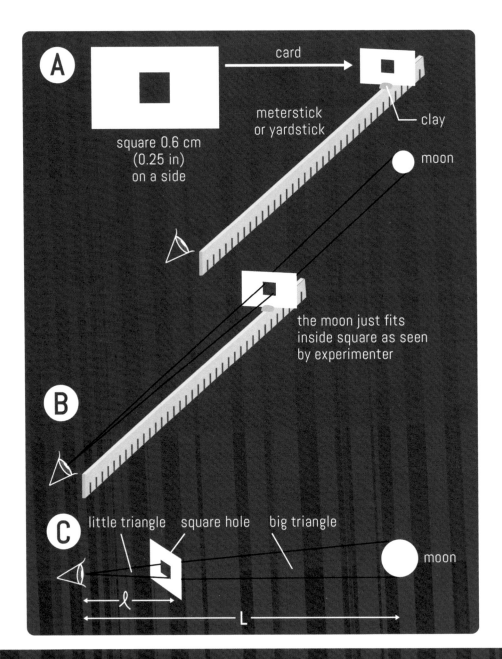

Figure 18. How big is the moon? a) Cut a ¼-inch-square (0.6-cm-sq) hole in a file card. Use clay to mount the card on a yardstick or meterstick. b) Move the card along the stick until the moon fits just inside the square hole. c) The little triangle from your eye to the square is part of the big triangle from your eye to the moon. Therefore, l ÷ 0.6 cm = L ÷ diameter of the moon.

2. Cut out the square with scissors.

3. Use a small piece of clay to mount the file card near the end of a yardstick or meterstick as shown in Figure 18a.

4. Start with the card on the far end of the stick, so that the moon fits easily inside the square. Hold one end of the stick close to your eye. Turn the other end toward the moon.

5. Slowly move the card toward your eye along the stick until the moon fits just inside the square, as shown in Figure 18b. The length of the square now matches the diameter (width) of the moon.

6. As you can see from Figure 18c, the little triangle between your eye and the square in the file card is a part of the big triangle between your eye and the moon. As a result, the length of the little triangle divided by its base (0.6 cm or 1/4 inch) is the same as the distance to the moon divided by the moon's diameter.

7. You can find the length of the little triangle divided by its base. It is the distance from the end of the stick (where your eye was) to the file card, divided by the length of the square hole (0.6 cm or 1/4 inch). For example, if the card were 72 cm (or 30 inches) away from your eye, then that length divided by 0.6 cm (or 1/4 inch) would be:

72 cm/0.6 cm = 120, or 30 in/0.25 in = 120.

As you can see, the result is the same whether you use centimeters or inches. This calculation shows that the length of the big triangle (390,000 km or

242,000 miles) divided by its base (the moon's diameter) is also 120. If the distance to the moon is 120 times its diameter, then dividing its distance by 120 should give us its diameter.

390,000 km/120 = 3,250 km, or 242,000 mi/120 = 2,000 mi.

What is the diameter of the moon according to your measurements?

EXPERIMENT 13

THE LIGHT FROM DISTANT SOURCES, SUCH AS STARS

By doing this experiment, you will see that light rays from distant sources, such as stars, are parallel.

THINGS YOU WILL NEED

- **clear lightbulb with a line filament**
- **socket for bulb**
- **common pins**
- **sheet of cardboard**
- **sunlight**

1. Figure 19 shows you how a clear lightbulb with a line filament can be used to represent a star. The bulb is placed in a socket and turned so that the end of the filament is turned toward you. The end of the

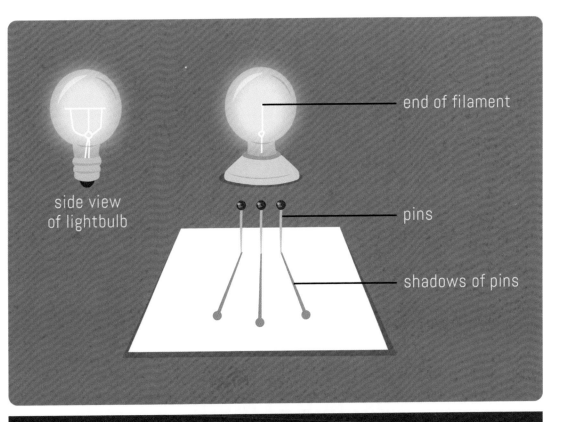

side view
of lightbulb

end of filament

pins

shadows of pins

Figure 19. The end of a line filament looks like a point of light—so it can be used to represent the light from a star. Shadows of pins can be used to show that the light rays that reach Earth from a given star are parallel.

filament is just a point of light. The same is true of a distant star. It is just a small dot set in the dark sky.

2. Stick three common pins side by side about a centimeter apart at one end of a sheet of cardboard. If you hold the pins close to the point of light, you will see that the shadows of the pins diverge (spread apart). But what happens as you move the pins farther from the light?

As you have just seen, light rays from a source of light that is far away (and not very far away at that) are parallel (or very nearly so) and, therefore, cast parallel shadows. What do you think will happen if these pins are placed in sunlight? Do you think their shadows will be parallel? How about light from the moon?

Try it! Were you right?

EXPLORING ON YOUR OWN

- Design and carry out an experiment to estimate the number of stars that are visible in the night sky.

EXPERIMENT 14

WATCHING THE MOON BY
DAY AND BY NIGHT

You will find it useful to record data about the moon in a notebook. A good time to begin your observations is a day or two after a new moon. A new moon occurs when the

THINGS YOU WILL NEED

- **time of the new moon**
- **notebook**
- **pen or pencil**

moon is between Earth and the sun. On rare occasions, it is positioned directly between the two, its shadow falling on Earth and creating an eclipse of the sun. You can usually find information about a new moon on the internet, in the weather section of a newspaper, or in an almanac. Several days after a new moon, look for the moon as the sun sets.

You can look at the moon as much as you want, but **never look directly at the sun. It can damage your eyes!**

1. Each time you observe the moon, record in a notebook the date, the time, and a drawing that shows the apparent shape of the moon. You should also record the direction in which you find the moon—north (N), south (S), east (E), west (W), or a direction in between, such as southwest (SW). Record, too, the moon's altitude above the horizon and, if possible, use fists to measure the distance—angle—between moon and sun.

   Distances and altitudes in the sky are usually measured in degrees. Sometimes, the sun and the moon appear close together in the sky. They might be less than 20 degrees apart. But the sun and the moon are actually about 150 million kilometers (93 million miles) apart. Since the moon orbits Earth, its average distance from the sun is the same as Earth's. So when someone says that the moon is close to the sun, they mean that the angle between the moon and the sun in the sky is small and are not referring to the actual distance between them.

2. You can make good estimates of angles using your fists. If you hold your fist at arm's length as shown in Figure 20, it will cover approximately 10 degrees

in the sky. To see that each fist is equal to about 10 degrees, start with the fist of one arm closed and extended toward the horizon (azimuth). Place fist upon fist, moving upward, as shown in the drawing, until one arm points straight up. You will find that it takes just about nine fists to reach this point. Since the angle between the horizon and the zenith straight overhead is 90 degrees, each fist must cover about 10 degrees: 90 degrees/9 = 10 degrees.

3. To find the angular distance between sun and moon, cover the sun with one of your hands. Then find how many fists separate the sun and the moon. Record the angle in your notebook. A typical record for one observation in this experiment is shown in Figure 20.

4. On each clear evening for the next few days, try to observe the moon at about the time of sunset. Make the same measurements you made before and record them in your notebook.

5. Also look for the moon early in the morning before sunrise, and at other times of the day and night. Record all your observations in your notebook.

6. What happens to the shape of the moon as days pass? What happens to the distance (angle) between the moon and the sun from one day to the next? What happens to the moon's location in the sky at sunset as days pass? Is the moon moving more to the east or to the west of the sun as days go by? What does this tell you about the time that the moon rises? Is it rising earlier or later each day?

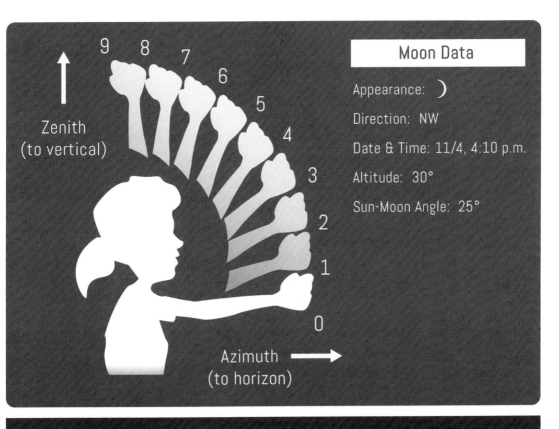

9 8 7
6
5
4
3
2
1
0

Zenith
(to vertical)

Azimuth
(to horizon)

Moon Data

Appearance:)

Direction: NW

Date & Time: 11/4, 4:10 p.m.

Altitude: 30°

Sun-Moon Angle: 25°

Figure 20. Hold your fist at arm's length, making the top of your fist even with the horizon. Then stack fist upon fist until one fist is directly over your head. You will find that you have gone 9 fists to cover the 90 degrees from the horizon to overhead. This means that your fist at arm's length covers about 10 degrees of sky. The sample data on the right shows one observation of the moon.

7. About two weeks after a new moon, if it is clear, you will see a full moon. Where is the sun when you see a full moon rising?

8. Keep recording data about the moon as far into the evening as possible. Can you see the moon the next morning when you awaken? Through approximately how many degrees does the moon move in one hour?

How might you estimate the distance (angle) between the sun and moon after the sun has set?

9. When the moon is no longer visible at sunset, begin looking for it early in the morning—before, during, and after sunrise. What happens to the moon's shape? Which side of the moon (left or right) is now the brighter side? Is this the side nearer or farther from the sun?

10. Continue your observations of the moon for several months. You should begin to see a pattern to the moon's motion and changing appearance. How much time passes between one full moon and the next? Does the full moon always rise in the same place (direction) on the horizon?

EXPLORING ON YOUR OWN

- Jupiter, the largest planet in our solar system, has many moons. You can see some of them by using binoculars. Perhaps you will have the same thrill Galileo experienced when he first saw Jupiter's moons. Seeing that these moons orbited Jupiter, he realized that Earth, too, might be orbiting the sun. How many moons of Jupiter can you see? How will you be able to tell that they go around the planet?

- Do some research to find out how many moons orbit each of the planets in our solar system. Are there any planets that have no moons?

EXPERIMENT 15

A MODEL OF MOON, EARTH, AND SUN

Scientists often make models to explain what they observe and the data they collect. In some cases, the theory can be illustrated by a physical model. In this experiment, you will examine a physical model of the moon, the sun, and Earth to see if it agrees with the data you have collected and the observations you have made.

THINGS YOU WILL NEED

- **dark room**
- **lamp and bright lightbulb**
- **partner**
- **a light-colored ball, about 2 inches in diameter, mounted on a stick or nail (a Styrofoam ball works well)**

1. To begin, put a single bright lightbulb at one end of a dark room. The lightbulb represents the sun.
2. Ask a partner to stand beside you and hold a white Styrofoam ball mounted on a stick. If the ball is made of Styrofoam, the stick can be pushed into the ball. If you can't find a Styrofoam ball, use an old tennis ball mounted on a long nail. Have your partner stand to your left while you face the light as shown in Figure 21.

Figure 21. This model represents Earth, the moon, and the sun.

In this model, your head represents Earth and the light-colored ball represents the moon. Since you are facing the sun (the light), the model now represents Earth at noon, when the sun is in the middle of its path across the sky. The position of the moon (Styrofoam ball) represents the east.

3. Slowly turn your head and body toward the moon in the east. Turning, your head represents Earth as it

rotates on its axis. In your model, you are seeing the moon rise.

4. After making a one-quarter turn, the sun (lightbulb) will be on your right (west). The time is sunset. The moon is directly in front of you, in the middle of the sky.

5. Figure 22a shows Earth (your head), the moon (ball), and the sun (lightbulb) in your model from above (overhead). Your head (Earth) is facing the moon after one-quarter turn—representing six hours of the day. Half the moon is lit by the sun, and the other half is dark. The moon is at first quarter. Have you ever seen the moon when it looked like this? If you have, at what angle was it from the sun?

6. Continue to turn slowly to your left to represent a rotating Earth. You will see the moon set after another quarter turn.

7. As you continue to slowly rotate, you will see the sun rise and move slowly across the "sky." Then you will again face the moon.

8. In the next part of the model, start at the position shown in Figure 22a, with the moon at first quarter. The moon moves slowly around Earth. After a week, the moon will move to a point on the opposite side of Earth from the sun. To represent this model, have your partner slowly move the moon (ball) a quarter of the way around you while you make seven complete rotations, representing a week. Watch what happens

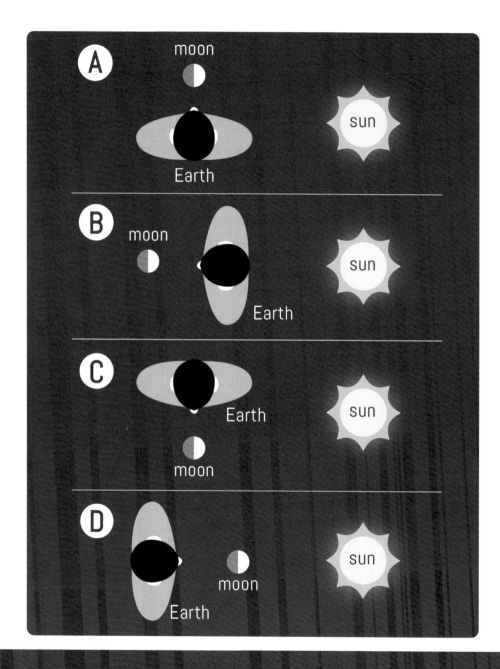

Figure 22. The model can be used to show the position of the moon at: first quarter, full moon, third quarter, and new moon.

to the moon's appearance as you make these turns. When you face the moon now (Figure 22b), it will be a full moon. If the moon is in the shadow of your head—an eclipse—have your partner raise the ball.

9. During another seven turns of Earth, the moon will move slowly to the position shown in Figure 22c. At this point, only half of the moon is bright (last quarter). After another seven turns of Earth, the moon will lie between Earth and the sun (Figure 22d). Since no reflected light can reach you, you will not see the moon. It is a new moon, at a position between sun and Earth.

Of course, a room is not a perfect model of space. Some light reflected by the walls and ceiling reaches the ball. This makes the dimly lit ball visible. In the space around the real moon, there are no walls or ceilings to reflect light, so light can't be seen. The lit side faces the sun.

10. Give your partner a chance to be the rotating Earth while you move the moon.

ABOUT THE MODEL

A good model will agree with what is found in the real world. Does the model you have just examined agree with the observations of the moon that you made? Did the real moon change from a thin crescent to a half moon, to a full moon? Did it then, after a week, appear as another half moon? Over the following week, did it again become a crescent—reversed—and then disappear before returning as a thin crescent near sunset?

If your answers to these questions are all yes, then the model is a good one. According to the model, as Earth rotates on its axis, the moon moves around Earth about once each month.

EXPLORING ON YOUR OWN

- What is a "blue moon"? What is meant by the phrase, "once in a blue moon"?
- Although lunar satellites have photographed all sides of the moon, only astronauts have actually seen the far side of the moon. Design a model to explain why we always see the same side of the moon.

EXPERIMENT 16

THE MOON'S ORBIT AROUND EARTH AND SUN

The moon orbits Earth in about four weeks (actually, 27.3 days). Since Earth orbits the sun, the moon must also follow a path around the sun. You might think that the moon's path

THINGS YOU WILL NEED

- **tape**
- **wrapping paper**
- **meterstick**
- **string**
- **a friend**
- **pencil or marking pen**
- **protractor**

around the sun is like the one shown in Figure 23a. But the actual path of the moon is quite different.

1. To see what the moon's orbit around the sun looks like, you can make a scale model. Earth is approximately 150,000,000 km from the sun. The distance between moon and Earth is approximately 400,000 km. The distances vary slightly because the orbits are not perfect circles, but elliptical.

2. To make a scale drawing of part of the orbits of Earth and the moon around the sun, let one centimeter represent one million kilometers. Then, Earth's orbit will have a radius of 150 centimeters (1.5 meters).

3. To draw part of this orbit, tape together some large sheets of wrapping paper. The final sheet of paper should be a square of about 1.6 m (5 ft 3 in) on a side.

4. Let the lower left-hand corner of the paper represent the position of the sun.

5. Cut a piece of string a little longer than 1.5 m.

6. Have a friend hold one end of the string on the lower left-hand corner of the paper.

7. Hold a pencil or marking pen against the string at a point 150 cm from the end your friend is holding. Using the string as a radius, draw the representation of Earth's orbit as shown in Figure 23b.

8. Next, using a protractor and the meterstick, draw radii from the sun to Earth at 0 degrees, 30 degrees, 60 degrees, and 90 degrees. Since Earth travels 360

degrees around the sun in one year, it will travel about 30 degrees in one month (360 degrees divided by 12 months).

9. Start with Earth (E) on the starting radius at 0 degrees and the moon at a new moon position as shown in Figure 23b. Since the moon (M) is about 400,000 km from Earth, it will be 4 mm (0.4 cm) closer to the sun than Earth. This distance is too small to show on the scale drawing in Figure 23b—so the distances shown between moon and Earth in the drawing are larger than they should be.

10. Mark Earth's position at one-week intervals as shown. Remember: the moon moves one quarter of the way around Earth about every seven days. So, seven days after the new moon, the moon has traveled clockwise around Earth to be a first quarter moon. The moon will move to positions representing new moon (start), first quarter, full moon, third quarter, new moon, and so on.

11. Mark Earth's and the moon's positions at weekly intervals for the three-month section of Earth's orbit you have drawn. Then connect the moon's successive positions with a dotted line. You now have a good representation of one-quarter of the moon's orbit about the sun. Does it look like the orbital path shown in Figure 23b?

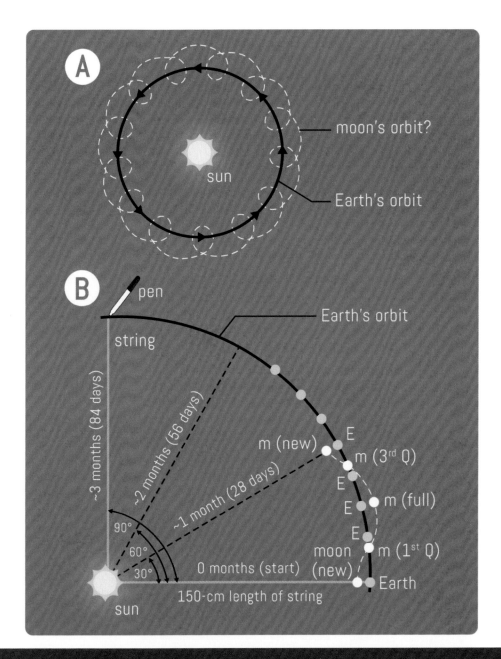

Figure 23. a) Is this diagram a good representation of the moon's path around the sun? b) Draw one-quarter of Earth's orbit to a scale of 1 cm for every 1,000,000 km. Then draw the moon's orbit around the sun as a dotted line. The moon on this scale will be 0.4 cm from Earth.

FROM ONE FULL MOON TO THE NEXT

The moon makes a complete orbit around Earth in approximately 27.3 days. The interval between one full moon and the next, however, is 29.5 days. As Figure 24 explains, when the moon has made one orbit, Earth has also moved about 27 degrees along its orbit. Consequently, the moon has to move along its orbit for another 2.2 days before it is again directly opposite the sun.

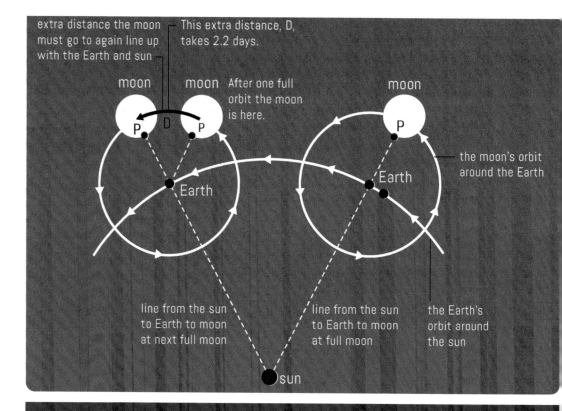

Figure 24. The moon makes a full orbit around Earth in about 27.3 days. Because Earth orbits the sun, however, the time from one full moon to the next is 29.5 days. The moon has to travel an extra distance (D) to make point (P) directly face Earth once again, lining up with Earth and the sun to create a full moon.

EXPERIMENT 17

A MODEL OF A LUNAR ECLIPSE

Occasionally, at the time of a full moon, Earth, moon, and sun lie along a line on the same plane, as shown in Figure 25a. Like any object in sunlight, Earth casts a shadow. We enter Earth's shadow every night after sunset. If the full moon enters that shadow, a lunar eclipse occurs.

THINGS YOU WILL NEED

- **scissors**
- **soda straw**
- **coin**
- **white card or pad**
- **frosted lightbulb, socket and electrical outlet**
- **dark room**
- **Styrofoam or clay balls 5 cm (2 in) and 1.3 cm (0.5 in.) in diameter**
- **stick 1.5 m (5 ft) long**
- **2 small finishing nails**
- **tape**

1. Shadows vary in darkness. To see this difference in darkness, use scissors to make a small slit in a soda straw.

2. Insert a coin in the straw. The straw can serve as a handle. Hold a white card or pad several feet from a glowing frosted lightbulb in an otherwise dark room.

3. Bring the coin near the card so that you see its dark shadow (umbra) on the paper.

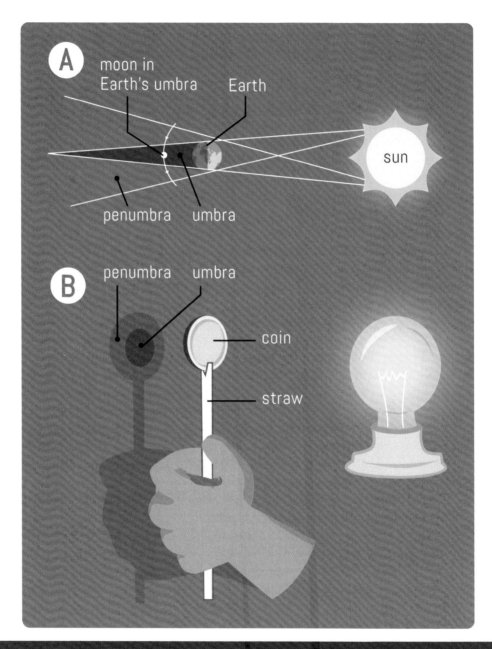

Figure 25. a) Earth casts a shadow. When the moon enters Earth's shadow, a lunar eclipse occurs. b) A coin casts a shadow. The dark part of the shadow is the umbra. No light from the bulb reaches the umbra. The lighter part of the shadow is the penumbra. Some light reaches the penumbra.

4. Slowly move the coin away from the card. The dark umbra grows smaller, while the fuzzy lighter shadow, the penumbra, grows larger (Figure 25b). As Figure 25 reveals, Earth's shadow has an umbra and a penumbra. If you examine the drawing carefully, you can see that some light from the sun reaches the penumbra. No direct sunlight reaches the umbra.

   The moon darkens as it enters Earth's penumbra and becomes much darker if it reaches the umbra. The darkened moon has a copper color, but it doesn't disappear. Earth's atmosphere bends a little of the sun's light around Earth so that some sunlight reaches the moon. Our view of the moon, then, is never totally blocked by Earth's shadow—even when the moon lies within the umbra of Earth's shadow.

5. Make a scale model of a lunar eclipse with a Styrofoam or clay ball about 5 cm (2 in) in diameter to represent Earth. Use another sphere with a diameter of 1.3 cm (0.5 in.). You will also need a stick 1.5 meters (5 ft) long, and two small finishing nails, one taped to each end of the stick (see Figure 26). The large ball represents Earth. The smaller ball represents the moon. The centers of "Earth" and the "moon" are about thirty Earth diameters apart. A stick 1.5 m (5 ft) long will separate "Earth" and "moon" by just about the distance needed for a scale model of the two spheres.

6. The real sun can serve as the sun in this model. It is much too far away to fit the scale. However, light rays

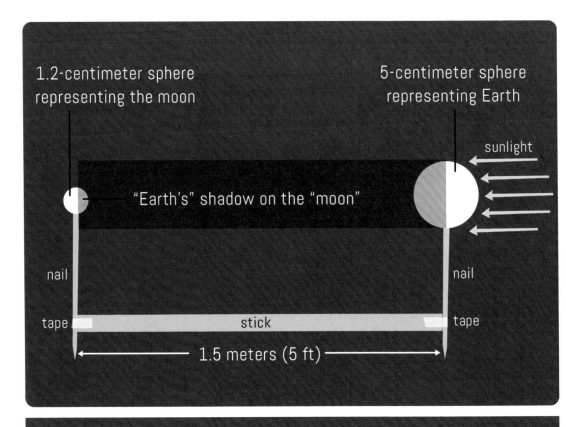

1.2-centimeter sphere
representing the moon

5-centimeter sphere
representing Earth

sunlight

"Earth's" shadow on the "moon"

nail

nail

tape

stick

tape

1.5 meters (5 ft)

Figure 26. Two spheres 1.5 m (5 ft) apart can be used to make a scale model of Earth and the moon. What conditions are needed to produce a lunar eclipse using this model?

reaching Earth from the sun are almost parallel—so its size and distance aren't important for this model.

7. Hold the stick so that "Earth" is closest to the sun. Tip and turn the stick until sun, "Earth," and "moon" are in line. When they are, Earth's shadow will fall on the moon. To see the moon move into and out of Earth's shadow, turn the stick slightly in a horizontal direction. How much do you have to tilt the stick to move the moon out of Earth's shadow? Why do you think an

eclipse does not occur at the time of every full moon? Save your model for the next experiment.

EXPLORING ON YOUR OWN

- Look at the shadow of a flagpole or telephone pole. Th shadow near the base of the pole is dark like an umbra. Farther out, the shadow shows a penumbra outside the umbra. If the shadow is long, its end may be fuzzy and light and have no umbra. How can you explain such a shadow? Does your shadow have a similar appearance?

EXPERIMENT 18

A MODEL OF A SOLAR ECLIPSE

You can use the model of a lunar eclipse that you used in Experiment 17 to model a solar eclipse.

1. Turn the model you used in the previous experiment so that the "moon" is closer to the sun than "Earth."

THINGS YOU WILL NEED

- **model you used in the previous experiment**
- **coin mounted on a soda straw used in the previous experiment**
- **frosted incandescent lightbulb and socket**
- **white file card or a white wall**

2. Move the stick until the moon's shadow falls on Earth. You now have a model of a solar eclipse, which occurs when the moon's shadow falls on Earth. During a solar eclipse, the sun, or part of it, is hidden by the moon. Because the moon is so small, its shadow covers only a small part of Earth's surface. The moon's shadow, like Earth's (and yours), has a dark

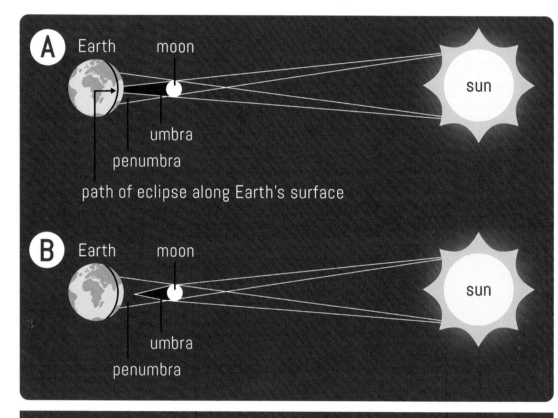

Figure 27. a) A solar eclipse occurs when the moon's shadow falls on Earth. If the umbra reaches Earth's surface, people in the umbra will see a total solar eclipse. That is, the sun will be completely blocked by the moon. Within the penumbra, there will be a partial eclipse. Only part of the sun will be blocked from view. b) If the umbra does not reach Earth's surface, there will not be a total eclipse anywhere on Earth's surface.

portion (umbra) and a fuzzy portion (penumbra). As Figure 27a shows, the umbra touches only a tiny part of Earth's surface. Only a small part of Earth will be covered by the moon's umbra. As Earth, the sun, and the moon move, the moon's umbra traces a narrow path across Earth's surface. The width of this shadow never exceeds 274 km (170 mi). Sometimes, only the penumbra reaches Earth's surface (Figure 27b). When that happens, part of the sun is always visible during the eclipse.

3. You can make another model of a solar eclipse that will show you what the sun looks like during a total and a partial solar eclipse. An ordinary frosted incandescent lightbulb can represent the sun. Use the coin mounted on the soda straw that you used in the previous experiment to represent the moon.

4. Stand several feet from the glowing lightbulb. Hold the coin in front of one eye and close your other eye. Move the coin back and forth until it covers all of the lightbulb. The entire bulb will disappear when the umbra of the coin's shadow falls on the pupil of your eye. The entire view of the bulb will be blocked from your eye. The coin (representing the moon) has totally eclipsed the bulb (sun).

5. Move the coin slightly to the side, and part of the bulb becomes visible. Part of your eye's pupil is in the coin's umbra and part is in its penumbra. In the same way, the moon casts a shadow on Earth during a solar eclipse. Where the shadow falls, it blocks from view

part of or all of the sun. **Do not do this experiment outdoors, using the real sun!**

6. Move the coin closer to your eye. Does it block out more or less of the bulb?

7. Slowly move the coin farther from your eye. Does the coin block out more or less of the bulb?

8. Hold the coin far enough away so that it blocks the center part of the lightbulb but leaves a ring of light around the edge. This is what happens during what is called an *annular solar eclipse.* In an annular eclipse, a thin ring of light is visible around the edge of the sun because the umbra part of the moon's shadow does not reach Earth's surface.

9. When the coin blocks out the top, bottom, or one side of the lightbulb, you have what happens during a partial eclipse when you are in the penumbra portion of the moon's shadow. Because the moon's umbra never stretches more than 274 km (170.26 mi) across Earth's surface, you are more likely to see a partial eclipse than a total eclipse.

10. Replace your eye with a white file card or a white wall to represent Earth's surface. Let the coin's shadow fall on the card or wall. You have an astronaut's view of Earth's surface during an eclipse. Can you find where there is a total eclipse? A partial eclipse? Can you move the coin so that no part of the umbra reaches the card or wall? What kind of an eclipse does this represent?

11. If you have an opportunity to view a solar eclipse, **never look at the sun!** Even during an eclipse, the sun is so bright it can severely damage your eyes. One way to view a solar eclipse is to make a pinhole image of the sun. Make a pinhole in one side of a large cardboard box. Turn the box so the pinhole faces the sun. With your back to the sun, place the box over your head. You can view the sun's image on a sheet of white paper taped to the side of the box opposite the pinhole. Sunlight entering the box through the pinhole will form an image of the sun on the screen.

12. Look under a leafy tree during an eclipse. You will see many pinhole images (sun dapples) of the eclipsed sun.

EXPLORING ON YOUR OWN

- Mercury and Venus sometimes come between the sun and Earth. Why don't they cause eclipses of the sun?

- If you look at the moon as it rises, it appears much larger than it does when it is higher in the sky. Is this an illusion? To find out, measure the diameter of a rising moon and compare it with the moon's diameter when it is higher in the sky.

CHAPTER FOUR

EARTH'S STAR: THE SUN

The ancient astronomer Aristarchus devised an ingenious way to measure the distance to the sun. He reasoned that when the moon is at first or last quarter and appears to be a half moon as shown in Figure 28, the sun's light must be striking the moon at 90 degrees to the line of sight of an observer on Earth (angle EMS). At that instant, he measured the angle between the moon's direction and the sun's direction (angle SEM). Angle SEM was very nearly 90 degrees, but not quite. Aristarchus estimated it to be 3 degrees shy of 90 degrees. It is actually 1/6 of a degree shy of 90 degrees. So his measurement of the distance to the sun (about 4.8 million miles [about 7.7 million km) was much too small. Using the actual 0.16-degree angle gives a distance of about 90 million miles (144,840,960 km).

EXPERIMENT 19

THE DIAMETER OF THE SUN

Earth is about 93 million miles from the sun. The distance varies some because Earth's orbit is elliptical. With that information and the materials listed, you can make a good estimate of the diameter of the sun.

THINGS YOU WILL NEED

- **2 thin, square sheets of cardboard**
- **yardstick**
- **a pin**
- **ruler**
- **notebook**
- **pen or pencil**

1. Hold a sheet of cardboard to which you have taped a piece of white paper at one end of a yardstick.
2. At the other end, hold another cardboard sheet in the center of which you have made a small hole with a pin. When sun, pinhole, and screen lie along a straight line, light from the sun passing through the pinhole will produce an image of the sun on the screen at the other end of the yardstick. (**Remember to never look directly at the sun. It can damage your eyes!**)
3. Use a ruler to measure the diameter of the sun's pinhole image.

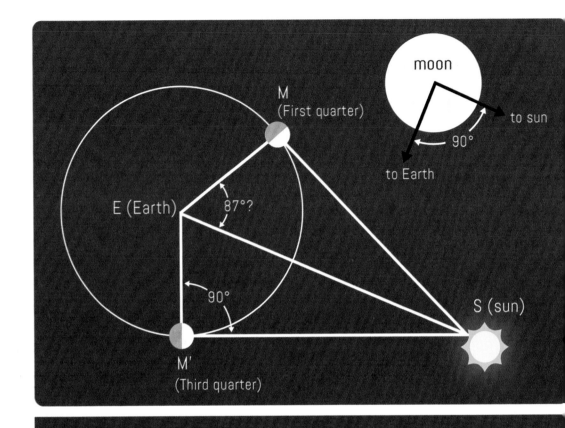

Figure 28. Aristarchus measured the distance to the sun using angle SEM, which he estimated to be 87 degrees. It is actually about 89.84 degrees.

4. As you can see from Figure 29, light rays from the sun pass through the pinhole to form the image, creating two similar triangles. This means that the ratio of the sun's diameter to its distance from the pinhole (93,000,000 mi) is the same as the ratio of the diameter of the image to the length of the yardstick.

5. You can calculate the ratio as the image's diameter divided by thirty-six inches. You can find the

diameter of the sun, therefore, in miles, which gives the same ratio when divided by 93,000,000.

$$d/l = D/L \text{ so } D = d/\,l \times L \ (93,000,000 \text{ mi})$$

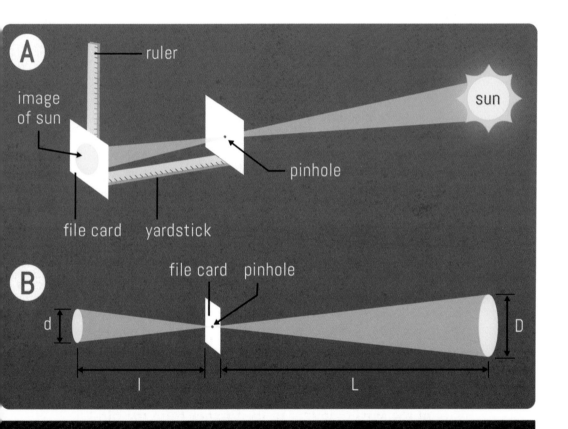

Figure 29. A pinhole, measurements, and a known distance to the sun will enable you to calculate the sun's diameter.

CHAPTER FIVE

OTHER PLANETS IN THE SOLAR SYSTEM

While we are not the only planet in the solar system, we may be the only one that harbors life. However, some recent observations indicate that there may be water on Mars. If that is true, we may eventually find living organisms or their remains on that planet.

BODE'S LAW

During the late 1700s, astronomers developed a number scheme that became known as *Bode's law*. If you write down the series of numbers "0, 3, 6, 12, 24, 48, 96…" and add 4 to each, then divide each by 10, you obtain: 0.4, 0.7, 1.0, 1.6, 2.8, 5.2, 10…

You may think these are just a bunch of random numbers, but the numbers are significant to astronomers, who often measure distances in astronomical units (AUs). One astronomical unit (AU) is the distance from Earth to the sun (93 million miles). If a planet were half as far from the sun as Earth, the radius of its orbit would be 0.5 AU. A planet twice as far from the sun as Earth would have an orbit with a radius of 2.0 AU.

Table 1 lists the planets and their orbital radii in astronomical units. Notice how closely the radii match Bode's law. You can see why astronomers found Bode's law significant.

Table 1 Some planets and the radii of their orbit in astronomical units (AU).

planet	Mercury	Venus	Earth	Mars	?	Jupiter	Saturn
radius (AU)	0.38	0.72	1.0	1.52	2.8	5.2	9.54

In 1781, the planet Uranus was discovered. It had a radius of 19.2 AU. This is close to the next number in the Bode's law series: $(192 + 4)/10 = 19.6$.

The radii of the planets, including Uranus, are close to the numbers in the Bode's law series, but there is no planet at 2.8. During the nineteenth century, astronomers began to find small bodies at about 2.8 AU from the sun in the region between Mars and Jupiter. These bodies, with diameters of 1,000 km (621 mi) or less, are known as asteroids. It used to be thought that the asteroids were the remnants of planets that exploded. But it is more likely that they are particles from the original solar system that never formed a planet.

Meteors are believed to be material left by comets that broke up as they moved around the sun. These particles continue to move along their comet's orbit—an orbit that crosses Earth's orbit, moving around the sun.

Occasionally, a comet becomes visible as it moves close to the sun. The orbits of comets are very long ellipses, unlike the nearly circular orbits of most planets.

A meteorite is a chunk of rock that has survived its fiery path through the atmosphere—striking Earth. Some meteorites have been huge. Once, a meteorite nearly 3 km (2 mi) in diameter struck Canada. An even larger one struck Central America about sixty-five million years ago. There is evidence that it created a huge cloud of dust-like particles that shielded the sun, causing Earth to cool. The lower temperature led to the extinction of the cold-blooded dinosaurs. Fortunately, such large meteorites are very rare.

EXPERIMENT 20

A SCALE MODEL OF THE SOLAR SYSTEM

From Experiment 19, you know that the diameter of the sun is about 1,392,082.56 km (865,000 miles). You also know that the distance from Earth to sun (the radius of Earth's orbit) is about 93,000,000 miles, and that the diameter of Earth is about 8,000 miles. Using this information and the data in Table 2, construct a scale model of the solar system. It will give you a good sense of the vast distances between planets.

Table 2: Information about planets in the solar system. Remember, the distance from Earth to sun is 1.0 AU.

Planet	Radius of orbit (AU)	Time to orbit Earth (years)	Diameter (Earth=1)	Mass (Earth=1)	Density (g/cm³)
Mercury	0.38	0.24	0.38	0.06	5.4
Venus	0.72	0.62	0.95	0.82	5.2
Earth	1.0	1.0	1.0	1.0	5.5
Mars	1.52	1.88	0.53	0.11	3.9
Jupiter	5.2	11.86	11.3	318	1.3
Saturn	9.5	29.46	9.44	95.2	0.7
Uranus	19.2	84.01	4.10	14.5	1.2
Neptune	30.1	164.8	3.88	17.2	1.7

A LOOK AT SOME PLANETS

After the moon, the brightest object in the night sky is Venus. It is often called the morning or evening star. Of course, it is not a star. Stars, like our sun, emit light. All the light we see from Venus, or any of the planets, is reflected sunlight. Because Venus is covered with clouds, 75 percent of the sunlight that strikes the planet is reflected. (Only 40 percent of the light striking Earth is reflected.) Since Venus's orbit is closer to the sun than ours, Venus never appears very far from the sun. Your newspaper—or the internet—will give you the rising and setting times for Venus so that you should have no trouble finding it in the morning, before sunrise, or in the evening, after sunset. If it happens to be close to the sun, you won't see it.

Watch Venus for several months. What is the largest angle it makes with the sun? You can use your fists to estimate this angle as the sun sets or rises. Again, a reminder: **never look directly at the sun!**

If you locate Venus just before sunrise and keep track of its position, you'll be able to see it even after the sun rises. It's fun to point it out to others and show them that a "star" can be seen even in the daytime.

Again, with the newspaper or internet to help you, you can probably locate the planet Jupiter, which is quite bright, and Mars, which has a reddish color. Mercury, which is never more than 28 degrees from the sun, and Saturn, the ringed planet, are more difficult to see. But with patience, you can find them. Binoculars will help, but if you're looking for Mercury, **don't look while the sun is in the sky** because Mercury is never far from the sun. Look for Mercury shortly after sunset or sunrise.

There are moons that orbit Jupiter, and you can see four of them with binoculars. To see them clearly, however, you will probably have to mount the binoculars on a tripod or hold them against a firm object.

On a clear, dark night you may see meteors, or shooting stars, as they are often called. These are particles of matter that burn up when they hit Earth's atmosphere. In certain places along Earth's orbit around the sun, these particles seem to be concentrated. When Earth crosses these places, you have an opportunity to see forty or fifty meteors per hour "shower" across the sky. The Perseid meteor shower can be seen best around August 12, and the Geminid meteor shower can be seen best around December 13. The showers are named for the constellation near where they appear in the sky. Most newspapers and television stations regularly report about these meteor showers shortly before they occur.

CHAPTER SIX

BEYOND THE SOLAR SYSTEM

Your scale model of the solar system probably made you aware of the vastness of the space between planets. But beyond the solar system are the stars, billions upon billions of them. How do scientists measure the distance to these stars? Astronomers use parallax to measure the distance to some of the nearer stars. Parallax is the apparent shift of one object with respect to another when observed from opposite ends of a baseline.

For example, hold one finger at arm's length in front of you. Hold a second finger about half as far from your face. Use the distance between your eyes as a baseline. Close first one eye, and then the other, having a partner hold one eye closed at a time if you can't wink with both eyes. You'll see the nearer finger shift position relative to the far finger.

Now put one finger on top of the other and again close one eye, and then the other. This time, the fingers remain together because they are at the same place.

EXPERIMENT 21

USING PARALLAX TO MEASURE A DISTANCE

This experiment will help you to understand how parallax can be used to measure distance.

Figure 30a shows a simple device you can build to measure distance using parallax.

> **THINGS YOU WILL NEED**
>
> - **sheet of cardboard**
> - **tape**
> - **3 common pins**
> - **measuring tape**

1. Tape a sheet of paper to the cardboard.
2. Find a distant object to use as one end of a sight line. The distant object might be a mountain peak, a steeple, a tall building, or something else several miles away. The nearer object, whose distance you will measure, could be a tree, a house, or a post a hundred or more yards from you. With the near and distant objects in line, use two pins to establish a sight line to the two objects (position 1 in Figure 30b).
3. Use a measuring tape to measure out a baseline of 30 to 40 meters perpendicular to your line of sight to the two objects.
4. Move to the other end of the baseline (position 2 in Figure 30b).

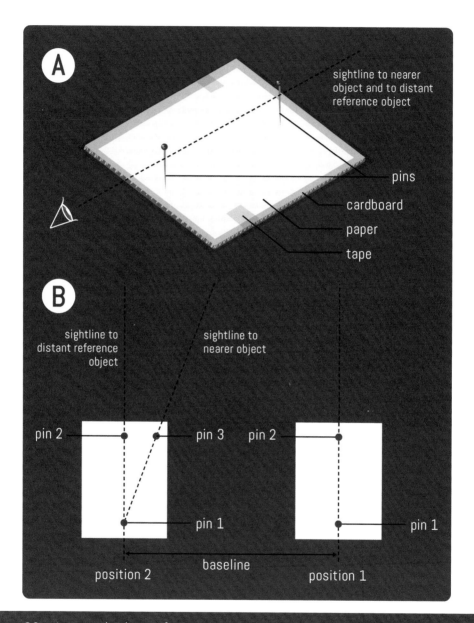

Figure 30. a) A simple device for measuring distance by means of parallax.
b) Establishing sight lines when the near and distant object are aligned (position 1)
at one end of a baseline and when they are not (position 2) at the other end of the
baseline. c) The triangle on the cardboard established by pins 1, 2, and 3 is similar
to triangle ABC on the ground where AB is the baseline. d) Even if the nearer and
more distant object do not initially lie on the same line of sight, the triangle on the
cardboard (123) is similar to the triangle on the ground (ABC).

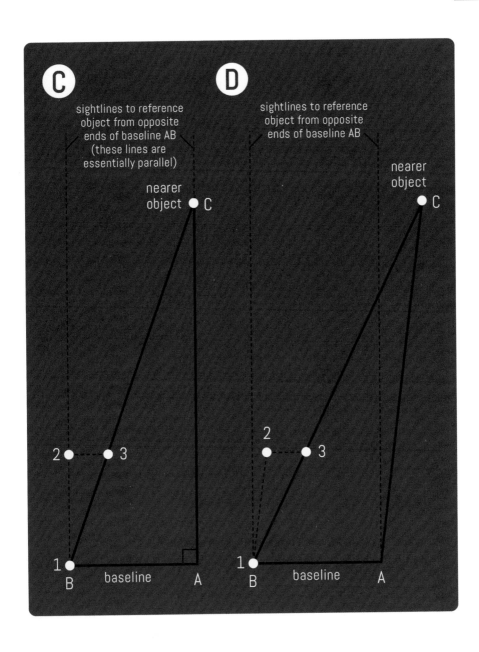

5. Again, find the line of sight along the two pins to the very distant object. Use the third pin (pin 3) and pin 1 to mark a new line of sight to the nearer object. Because of parallax, the nearer object has now shifted its apparent position relative to the more distant object.

   The triangle on the paper established by pins 1, 2, and 3 is similar to, but much smaller than the triangle on the ground (triangle ABC in Figure 30c).

6. By measuring the actual baseline and the smaller distances between pins 1 and 3 and pins 2 and 3 on the cardboard, you can determine the distance to the nearer object. The dotted lines to the distant reference object are essentially parallel because the reference object is so far away. According to your measurements, what is the distance to the nearer object? As Figure 30d reveals, you could find the distance to the nearer object, even if it were not possible to align it with the distant reference object.

USING PARALLAX TO MEASURE THE DISTANCE TO STARS

The distance to a nearer star can be measured using parallax. As Figure 31 shows, sight lines to a near star can be made at six-month intervals, when Earth is at opposite sides of its orbit. Measurements taken at these times

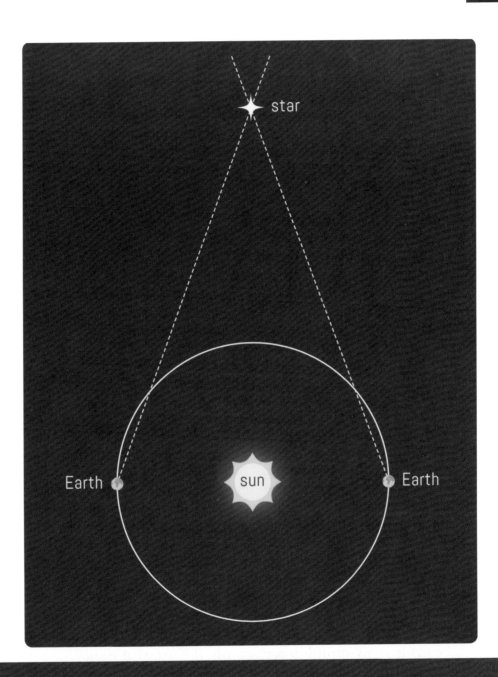

Figure 31. Scientists measure the distance to a star using parallax and the diameter of Earth's orbit as a baseline. (Not to scale.)

provide the largest baseline (2 AU, 300 million km, or 186 million miles).

The shift in the star's position relative to the very distant stars is angle x in Figure 31. All the angles measured to these stars are in seconds of arc. One degree contains 60 minutes (60') of arc and a minute contains 60 seconds (60") of arc.

Astronomers invented a unit, the parsec, to express the distance to stars. A parsec is the distance at which a star would have a parallax of one second of arc.

Table 3 shows some of the nearest stars and their distances in seconds of arc, parsecs, and light-years (the distance light travels in one year.) One parsec is equal to a distance of 3.26 light-years.

Table 3. The distances to some of the nearer stars

Star	Parallax (sec of arc)	Distance (parsecs)	Distance (light-years)
Proxima Centauri	0.763	1.31	4.27
Alpha Centauri	0.752	1.33	4.34
Bernard's Star	0.545	1.33	5.97
Sirius	0.375	2.67	8.70
61 Cygni	0.292	3.42	11.15

The distances to stars that are very far away require an understanding of the Hertzsprung-Russell diagram, which is beyond the scope of this book.

TYPES OF STARS

Stars are classified according to their surface temperature. Astronomers can determine a star's temperature by the type of light it emits. Red stars are cooler than blue stars as you can see from Table 3.

Table 4. Star types, temperature, and color.

Star Type	Temperature (°C)	Color	Example
O	>35,000	greenish or bluish-white	rare
B	10,000–35,000	hot white	Rigel in Orion
A	about 10,000	cool white	Sirius in Canus Major
F	6,000–10,000	slightly yellow	Polaris
G	about 6,000	yellow	our sun
K	about 4,000	orange	Arcturus in Boötes
M	about 3,000	red	Betelgeuse in Orion

EXPERIMENT 22

A SPECTROSCOPE

To examine the light emitted by stars, astronomers use spectroscopes. A spectroscope separates light into the various colors that make it up. Light has wavelike properties. Red light has longer wavelengths than blue light. To separate ordinary white light into its various colors or wavelengths, you can build a simple spectroscope.

1. Cut two square holes (1 in or 2.5 cm on a side) in opposite ends of a shoe box.
2. Cover one of the holes with two small pieces of cardboard so that they form a narrow slit.

THINGS YOU WILL NEED

- **knife or scissors**
- **shoe box**
- **cardboard**
- **tape**
- **diffraction grating (You can buy diffraction gratings in a hobby shop or online, or you can borrow one from your school's science department.)**
- **black construction paper**
- **clear tubular showcase bulb with a straight line filament or an unfrosted lightbulb**
- **large cardboard box**
- **white paper**
- **a partner**

3. Tape a piece of diffraction grating over the other hole. But before you tape it in place, hold it up toward a light. Turn it so that when light comes through the grating, it spreads out into a horizontal spectrum of colors.
4. Cover the inside of the box, except for the squares, with black construction paper. Then tape the box shut.
5. Hold the spectroscope so that the slit in the front of the box is parallel with the bright filament of a showcase lamp or an unfrosted lightbulb.
6. Look to either side as you view the light through the spectroscope's diffraction grating. You will see a spectrum containing all the colors of the rainbow.
7. Use your spectroscope to look at a fluorescent lightbulb such as one in a study lamp. You'll see not only a spectrum, but the bright violet, green, and yellow lines emitted by the mercury vapor inside the bulb. Like mercury, each element emits characteristic wavelengths or colors. Look at a neon light. What colors are emitted by neon? Using spectroscopes, astronomers can figure out what elements are in stars.
8. To see the colors in sunlight, cut a small hole in one side of a large cardboard box. The hole should be in the middle of the side near the bottom.
9. Tape a diffraction grating over the hole.
10. Tape a sheet of white paper to the inside of the box on the side opposite the hole.
11. Turn the box upside down and get inside with your back toward the diffraction grating. **Remember: Never look at the sun.** Have a partner help you turn

the box so that sunlight falls onto the grating. Look on the white screen to see the colors found in sunlight.

12. To view a solar eclipse, substitute a pin hole for the diffraction grating.

STARS AND THE DOPPLER EFFECT

When a star is coming toward us at high speed, the wavelengths of the light it emits are shorter than normal (a blue shift). When the star is traveling away from us, its light waves stretch into longer wavelengths (a red shift). This phenomenon is known as the Doppler effect. You've probably observed this effect with sound. If a car is approaching you with its horn blaring, the pitch seems higher than usual because the vibrations are more frequent. The sound waves are "squeezed" together because the horn is traveling toward you as they are emitted. One wave follows the next more closely than it would if the car were at rest. When the car passes you and moves away, the pitch seems to be lower. The car is moving away from the waves that strike your ear, so the waves are "stretched" and reach you less frequently than if the car were at rest.

Similarly, receding stars emit longer wavelengths of light than they would if they were at rest, creating a red shift— appearing more red. Approaching stars, on the other hand, show a blue shift as their wavelengths shorten. Knowing the speed of light and the degree of shift in a star's wavelengths, astronomers can determine the speed at which stars are moving toward or away from us. By comparing the red shifts or blue shifts of stars turning on their axes, they can tell which way a star is spinning. The observation of red shifts in galaxies has even provided good evidence that the universe is expanding—and that the farther a galaxy is from us, the faster it is moving away.

THE BIRTHS AND DEATHS OF STARS

As gravity pulls together the dark thin globs of dust in space, cold matter begins to get warmer. Eventually, temperatures rise and hydrogen begins to fuse to make helium at the core of the contracting matter. At this point, the pressure created by energy produced at the core is enough to balance the inward gravitational pressure, and the star becomes stable. If the contracting mass is less than 8 percent of our sun's mass, a solid, planet-like object will form. If the mass is greater than that of one hundred suns, the radiation emitted will prevent the contraction needed to ignite hydrogen and produce a star.

Big stars burn hydrogen faster than small stars. The lifetime of our sun is estimated to be about ten billion years. A star with half the mass of the sun would live for two hundred billion years. But one with a mass fifteen times that of the sun would burn out in only fifteen million years. The large stars are the O, B, and A stars in Table 4. Our sun is a type G star.

When all of the hydrogen in a star's core has burned, hydrogen in the shell around the core begins to burn. Contraction due to gravity within the core makes the core hotter, causing layers around the star to expand. As the star expands, its surface temperature falls to about 4,000 degrees Celsius or lower. Such stars, entering the last phases of their lives, emit red light and are called *red giants*. Betelgeuse, in the constellation Orion, is an example of a red giant.

In another five billion years, our sun will become a red giant, swelling until it swallows Mercury, Venus, and Earth, and vaporizes the atmospheres of the outer planets.

The core of an old star in its red giant stage is rich in helium because helium is the product of hydrogen fusion. As the red giant's core contracts, its temperature rises. When it reaches about 100,000,000 degrees, helium begins to burn (fuse), producing heavier elements. A star's helium takes only about one-tenth as long to burn as hydrogen does, so a star in the red giant stage is near the end of its life cycle. When the helium in the core has been consumed, a sequence similar to that following the burning of the hydrogen core takes place. The core contracts, and the temperature increases from the contraction, igniting the helium in the shell around the core. As it burns, the star expands again, producing a red super giant. Pulses of energy from the helium-burning core cause as much as half of a star's mass to be blown off into space.

Ejection of the outer layers of a dying star expose its hot core. Ultraviolet light emitted by the core may cause the ejected gases to glow, producing a planetary nebula. The Great Nebula in Orion can be seen as a misty patch just below the three stars that make up Orion's belt. With binoculars, you can see it quite clearly.

After puffing away much of its mass, the core of a low-mass star contracts to become a white dwarf. The matter in a white dwarf is packed together so tightly that it weighs about a million times as much as an equal volume of water.

As the star cools over billions of years, it grows dimmer, finally becoming a dense, cold, Earth-sized sphere.

Stars with masses greater than four times our sun's mass will contract again, raising temperatures to the point at which carbon fuses, forming neon, magnesium, oxygen, and helium. Still more massive stars will fuse neon and helium into magnesium, and oxygen into sulfur, phosphorus, silicon, and magnesium. Stars that are twenty-five or more times more massive than the sun will fuse silicon into iron—the end product of nuclear fusion.

Contraction of the core of such a large star squeezes matter until it is more than one hundred trillion times as dense as water. It is packed as tightly as the nuclei of atoms. When other contracting matter hits this dense core, it bounces off, producing a shock wave that blows the star apart.

A SUPERNOVA

As the outer layers of a large star are blown apart, the star's brightness increases by a factor of one hundred million in the course of seconds. The sudden appearance of such a bright star is called a *supernova*. The appearance of a supernova in the southern hemisphere on February 24, 1987, excited astronomers throughout the world. The Supernova 1987A (SN 1987A) was discovered by Ian Shelton of the University of Toronto. He was working at the Carnegie Institution's Las Campanas Observatory in Chile when he first saw the star. Though it burns with the brilliance of a billion suns and is clearly visible to the naked eye, it does not look as bright as many stars because it is so far away—170 thousand light-years. Despite this great distance, SN 1987A is the first visible supernova since 1885, and the brightest since 1604. It differs from other supernovas in a number of ways and is accompanied by an unexplained companion.

The core of a supernova consists of neutrons because electrons in the compressed matter have combined with protons to produce them. Physicists theorize that this core, which is a neutron star, should release neutrinos (tiny particles carrying little or no mass and no charge) as the supernova forms.

Sometimes, a star suddenly increases in brightness by a factor of a million. Such a star is called a *nova.* Novas are more common than supernovas. Astronomers think that they are formed when a white dwarf pulls matter from a larger companion star. As hydrogen is pulled inward by the smaller star, the temperature of the gas rises until it begins to undergo fusion, producing a gigantic hydrogen bomb.

BLACK HOLES

Calculations show that if a dying star is more than three times greater than the mass of the sun, the escape velocity (the speed needed to overcome gravity and leave the star) from this extremely dense body will be greater than the speed of light. This means that nothing, not even light, can escape from the dead star. Such dense objects are called *black holes*: *black* because no light can escape from them, and *holes* because anything coming close to the intense gravity falls into it.

There is further evidence indicating that black holes exist. Some stars orbit something invisible, something that must have an incredibly high density. Many astronomers believe that a region so dense and powerful must be a black hole. Astronomers at Ohio State University have evidence that leads them to believe that they have seen a star near the center of a galaxy being torn apart by a black hole.

Some astronomers suggest that black holes near the centers of galaxies may themselves coalesce into giant black holes that will "eat" anything that gets caught in their gravity.

QUASARS

During the late 1950s and early 1960s, radio astronomers— astronomers who detect objects in the sky using radio waves rather than light—discovered a number of objects that had very strange spectra. Some of these objects were called *quasi-stellar radio sources* because of their star-like appearance. This term was soon shortened to *quasars*. Analysis of the light and radio waves from these sources led astronomers to realize that the strange spectra resulted from huge red shifts. These red shifts indicated that quasars were farther away than anything that had ever been detected before—up to eighteen billion light-years. Further, quasars seemed to emit energies equal to a trillion suns even though they were no larger than our solar system.

To explain how an object as small as our solar system can emit energy equal to that of one hundred galaxies, some astronomers suggest that quasars are powered by super massive black holes. These black holes are surrounded by vast masses of gases that accelerate around the hole as they spiral inward before being swallowed.

COSMOLOGY AND THE ORIGIN OF THE UNIVERSE

As astronomers study the stars and galaxies in the space that surrounds us, their extensive observations of red shifts make it clear that the universe is expanding. One model of this expanding universe can be made by placing ink spots on a balloon. As the balloon is inflated, the spots get larger and grow farther apart. The farther one spot is from another, the faster they separate. Similarly, astronomers find that more distant galaxies seem to be experiencing greater red shifts; the farther they are from us, the more quickly their light waves lengthen.

The model of the expanding universe is often referred to as part of the Big Bang theory. At time zero, matter was infinitely dense and the laws of physics that we know today did not apply. Suddenly, the matter began to expand. It is this dramatic moment that is referred to as the *Big Bang*. After about a million years, expansion caused the temperature to drop to a point where matter, as we know it, could begin to form from primitive particles.

If the universe is dense enough, gravity will eventually stop this process of expansion, and the universe will contract back to its original state. Such a universe is said to be bounded or closed. Its contraction or Big Crunch will be followed by another Big Bang. If the density of the universe is equal to about three hydrogen atoms per cubic meter, then the universe will continue to expand—but at a rate approaching zero. If the density is any lower, the universe will continue to expand and can be understood to be unbounded or open.

When astronomers add up all of the mass in the matter they can see, they find that there does not appear to be a density high enough to prevent the universe from expanding forever. It appears to be unbounded. But astronomer Vera Rubin, who studies the rotation rate of galaxies, has found that the rotation of the outer parts of some galaxies cannot be explained unless there is more mass than is visible. Many astronomers believe that the extra mass exists as dark matter—gas, rocks, or black holes. Some believe that it takes the form of neutrinos, though recent evidence indicates that neutrinos probably have no mass.

Though we may eventually know whether the universe is open or closed, astronomers do not know if we will ever know the origin of the matter or energy that led to the Big Bang.

GLOSSARY

azimuth The direction of a celestial object from an observer, expressed as the angular distance from the north point of the horizon.

constellation A group of stars commonly understood to resemble a familiar shape.

Foucault pendulum An experimental tool of Jean Foucault, a French physicist, who used a very long, heavy pendulum to show that Earth rotates. Over hours of time, the path of his pendulum slowly changed as Earth rotated beneath it. He put to rest the idea that the stars and sun rotated around Earth.

full moon A phase of the moon in which its entire Earth-facing side is illuminated by the sun.

latitude Positions north or south of the equator as measured in degrees. Lines of latitude surround Earth.

light-year The distance light travels in one year.

longitude Positions east or west of the prime meridian (Greenwich, England) as measured in degrees from 0 to 180.

lunar eclipse A shadow cast by Earth that may cover all or part of the moon when Earth is positioned directly between the moon and the sun.

new moon A phase of the moon when it is directly between Earth and the sun and cannot be seen from Earth.

north polar constellations Constellations that are near and around Polaris.

orbit The elliptical path followed by a planet—or another celestial object—around a star, moon, or planet.

parallax The apparent shift of one object with respect to another when observed from opposite ends of a baseline.

parsec A measurement of distance used by astronomers. One parsec is the distance at which a star would have a parallax of one second of arc.

Polaris The North Star, which is almost directly above Earth's North Pole.

seasons The changes in temperature and hours of sunlight that take place due to the tilt of Earth's axis as Earth moves along its orbit.

solar eclipse A shadow cast by the moon onto Earth when it lies directly between Earth and the sun.

FURTHER READING

BOOKS

Dickinson, Terence. *NightWatch: A Practical Guide to Viewing the Universe.* Richmond Hill, Canada: Firefly Books, 2006.

Golden, Leslie M. *Laboratory Experiments in Physics for Modern Astronomy: With Comprehensive Development of the Physical Principals.* New York, NY: Springer Publishing, 2012.

Greeve, Tom. *Astronomers.* North Mankato, MN: Rourke Educational Media, 2016.

Hamen. Susan. *Astronomy in the Real World.* Minneapolis, MN: Abdo Publishing Company, 2016.

Hirshfield, Alan W. *Parallax: The Race to Measure the Cosmos.* Mineola, NY: Dover Publications, 2013.

Holt, Geoff. *Project Earth Science: Astronomy.* Arlington, VA: NSTA Press, 2011.

Prinja, Raman. *Night Sky Watcher.* Lake Forest, CA: QEB, 2016.

Tiner, John Hudson. *Exploring the World of Astronomy: From Center of the Sun to Edge of the Universe.* Green Forest, AZ: New Leaf Publishing, 2013.

WEBSITES

Astronomy **Magazine**
astronomy.com
A website loaded with links to news, blogs, and more websites devoted to astronomy.

NASA
nasa.gov
News, images, and videos from America's space agency.

Space.com
space.com
News on astronomy and space exploration.

CAREER INFORMATION

American Astronomical Society

aas.org/learn/careers-astronomy

Read about where astronomers work and where their jobs are.

Big Future

bigfuture.collegeboard.org/careers/science-physicists-astronomers

A career- and job-based website with a focus on college majors.

International Astronomical Union

iau.org/public/themes/careers

Find out what it takes to be an astronomer.

Science Pioneers

sciencepioneers.org/students/stem-websites

Links to various STEM career websites.

WITHMYDEGREE.org

withmydegree.org/can-astronomy-degree

Offers ideas for what you might do with an astronomy degree.

INDEX

A

adult, working with a, 14, 15, 18
Aldebaran, 29
Antares, 30
Arctic Circle, 22
Arcturus, 30
Aristarchus, 92
asterisms, 17
asteroids, 8, 12, 97
astrolabe, 38
astrology, 8
astronomers
  about, 8
  how to become, 9–11
  scientific method and, 12–14
  specializations, 10
  what they do, 11–12
astronomical units, 96–97
astronomy
  defined, 8
  early, 8, 17, 40, 55, 57, 61, 72,
    92
astrophysicists, 8–10
Auriga, 29
autumn, constellations to see
    during, 29

B

Betelgeuse, 114
Big Bang theory, 118–119
Big Dipper, 18–20, 24, 25, 26, 29,
    37
black holes, 116–118
Bode's law, 96–97
Bootes, 30

C

Canis Major, 29
Capella, 29
Cassiopeia, 23, 24, 29, 30
Castor, 30
celestial hemisphere, 42, 48
celestial sphere, 48
Cepheus, 23, 29, 30
college/university, 9–10
comets, 8, 98
compass, magnetic, 21–22
constellations, 17–34, 101
  definition of, 17
  experiments about, 18–25
  watching over the seasons, 29–30
cosmic background microwave
    radiation, 8
Cygnus, 29, 30

D

Deneb, 29
dependent variable, 13
dipper constellations, 17, 18–20,
    30
Doppler effect, 112–113
Draco, 23
Dubhe, 19, 37

E

Earth, 12, 17, 20, 22, 35–59, 97,
    100, 101, 114
  atmosphere, 57–58
  distance from moon, 61–63
  distance from sun, 92, 99
  experiments about, 37–42,

44–54, 59
  lunar eclipse and, 55, 83–87
  model of, 73–78
  orbit around sun, 28, 29, 40–43,
    60, 72, 78, 93, 101
  positions on, 35, 43
  solar eclipse and, 68, 87–91
  as a sphere, 55–57
  turns on axis, 26, 42, 52–54, 57,
    60, 78
eclipse
  annular solar eclipse, 90
  lunar, 55, 83–87
  solar, 68, 87–91
equator, 24, 35, 43, 57
Eratosthenes, 55–57
experiments
  before you begin, 14
  controlled, 13
  safety and, 14–16

F

Foucault, Jean, 40, 43, 57
Foucault pendulums, 40–42, 57

G

galaxies, 8, 10, 12, 113, 117, 118,
  119
Galileo, 40, 72
gamma rays, 12
  bursts, 8
Gemini, 30
Geminid meteor shower, 101
Graduate Record Examination
  (GRE), 10
graduate school, 9, 10–11
Great Nebula, 114
Greenwich, England, 35, 43

H

high school, 9, 10
hypothesis, 12–13

I

independent variable, 13
infrared radiation, 12

J

Jupiter, 60, 72, 97, 100–101

L

latitude, 35, 37–38, 43, 57
light, color of, 11–12
light rays, 63, 66–68, 94
Little Dipper, 18, 19–20
longitude, 35, 43

M

magnetic compass, 21–22
Mars, 96, 97, 100
Merak, 19, 20, 37
Mercury, 91, 100, 114
meridians, 43
meteorites, 98
meteors, 98, 101
microwaves, 12
middle school, 9
moon, the, 40, 42, 55, 57, 60–91,
  92, 99
  eclipse of, 55, 83–87
  experiments about, 63–91
  full moon, 71, 72, 77, 82, 83
  measuring distance to, 61–63
model of, 73–78
  new moon, 68–69
  observing over time, 68–72

orbit around Earth, 78–82
path of, 61, 78–79
phases of, 77–78
size of, 63–66
solar eclipse and, 68, 87–91
moons, 8, 60, 72, 101

N
nebulae, 8, 17, 114
north, finding true, 21–22
Northern Cross, 29
northern sky, 17, 18
north polar constellations
    finding, 22–23, 24, 26–28, 30
    observing over time in hours, 24, 26
    observing over time in months, 25
North Pole, 17, 20, 21–22, 37, 43
    magnetic, 22
North Star, 18, 20, 37, 38, 57
novas, 116

O
Orion, 17, 30, 114

P
parallels, 43
parallax, 102
    to measure distance, 103–109
partner, working with a, 14, 20, 38
Pegasus, 29
penumbra, 85, 87, 89, 90
Perseid meteor shower, 101
PhD, 8, 9, 10
photons, 12
planets, 8, 10, 12, 42, 60, 72, 96–101

Pleiades, 30
Polaris, 17, 18, 20, 21, 22, 23, 24, 26, 37–38, 57
Pollux, 30
prime meridian, 43

Q
quasars, 117–118

R
radiation, 11–12
radio waves, 12, 117
red giants, 114
red shift, 112–113, 117, 118
research, 8, 9, 11, 12
Rubin, Vera, 119

S
safety, 14–16
Sagittarius, 30
satellites, 12, 55, 60
Saturn, 100
scattering, 58, 59
scientific method, 12–14
Scorpius, 30
seasons
    explaining, 52–54
    watching constellations over, 29–30
Shelton, Ian, 115
shooting stars, 101
Sirius, 29
sky, 42, 48
    why it's blue, 57–58, 59
solar system, 12, 35, 72
    beyond the, 102–119
    planets in the, 96–101

scale model experiment of,
    98–101
spectroscope, 110–112
spectrum, visible, 12
Spica, 30
spring, constellations to see during,
    30
stars, 8, 11, 17, 18–20, 26, 28, 29,
    30, 37–38, 42, 57, 58, 100,
    102
  births and deaths of, 113–115
  Doppler effect and, 112–113
  examining light emitted by,
    110–112
  types of, 109, 113
  using parallax to measure
    distance to, 106–109
summer, constellations to see
    during, 30
sun, the, 10, 26, 28, 35, 55, 57,
    58, 60–61, 68, 92–95, 97, 98,
    100, 114
  diameter of, 93–95, 98
  distance to, 92, 99
  Earth's rotation around, 40–43
  experiment about, 93–95
  model of, 73–78
  path of, 44–47, 48–51, 52
  rising/setting of, 60
  solar eclipse, 68, 87–91
sundial, 44–47
sunsets, 58, 59
supernovas, 8, 115–116

T

Taurus, 29
telescope, 11, 12
time zones, 43
true north, 21–22

U

ultraviolet light, 12, 114
umbra, 83, 85, 87, 89, 90
Uranus, 97
Ursa Major, 18
Ursa Minor, 18

V

variables, 13
Venus, 42, 91, 99–100, 114
Virgo, 30

W

white dwarf, 114, 116
winter, constellations to see during,
    29–30

X

X-rays, 12